MODERN LEGAL STUDIES

STRICT AND VICARIOUS LIABILITY
A STUDY IN ADMINISTRATIVE CRIMINAL LAW

by
L. H. LEIGH, B.A., LL.B. Ph.D.

Professor of Law in the University of London
London School of Economic and Political Science

LONDON
SWEET & MAXWELL
1982

Published in 1982 by
Sweet & Maxwell Limited of
11 New Fetter Lane, London.
Computerset by Promenade Graphics Limited, Cheltenham
and printed in Great Britain by
J. W. Arrowsmith Limited, London and Bristol.

British Library Cataloguing in Publication Data
Leigh, L. H.
Strict and vicarious liability.—(Modern legal studies)
1. Liability
I. Title   II. Series
344.2063'8   KD1983

ISBN 0–421–267607
ISBN 0–421–267704 Pbk

MODERN LEGAL STUDIES

STRICT AND VICARIOUS LIABILITY

A STUDY IN
ADMINISTRATIVE CRIMINAL LAW

90 0748436 2

AUSTRALIA
The Law Book Company Ltd.
Sydney : Melbourne : Brisbane

CANADA AND U.S.A.
The Carswell Company Ltd.
Agincourt, Ontario

INDIA
N. M. Tripathi Private Ltd.
Bombay
and
Eastern Law House Private Ltd.
Calcutta and Delhi
M.P.P. House
Bangalore

ISRAEL
Steimatzky's Agency Ltd.
Jerusalem : Tel Aviv : Haifa

MALAYSIA : SINGAPORE : BRUNEI
Malayan Law Journal (Pte.) Ltd.
Singapore

NEW ZEALAND
Sweet & Maxwell (N.Z.) Ltd.
Auckland

PAKISTAN
Pakistan Law House
Karachi

PREFACE

THIS essay is an attempt to examine from a functional perspective topics conventionally dealt with as strict and vicarious liability. It seeks to examine their role in the context of what might be called administrative criminal law, and it looks in particular at the terms upon which liability is imposed and defences granted as well as the way in which the law is enforced in practice. This seemed an appropriate time to draw the attention of students to a series of empirical studies which have begun to consider the way in which regulatory legislation is enforced in fact. Because this essay is introductory, and rather tentative in character, it has been necessary to treat material selectively. It does not purport to deal with all the issues which pertain to the field; it does not for example treat in detail of mistake of fact or status offences, or various projects of reform which have been proposed in the United States and the Commonwealth, neither is it fully comparative. It certainly does not discuss all the English cases, nor all the statutes. I have instead sought to discuss the principal issues concerned in sufficient detail and with sufficient reference to authority to place before students what I hope is a defensible, readable and sufficiently documented thesis to provide a basis for debate. To rehabilitate strict and vicarious liability completely is neither possible nor desirable, but one can at least suggest a different emphasis to that which is commonly found in treatments of the subject, and virtues which are often not sufficiently recognised.

I owe thanks above all to Professor Edward Griew of the University of Leicester and to my colleague, Professor W. R. Cornish, for reading the entire manuscript. Their scrutiny was invaluable. Publishers are by now used to praise for their tact, courtesy, forbearance and efficiency—but they deserve it.

December 1981   L. H. LEIGH

ERRATUM

*On page 5 the passage immediately following th[e]
quotation should read:*

"In addition there is widespread agreement amon[g]
scholars that general defences such as duress, automatism and insanity apply to offences of stri[ct]
liability.[17] Necessity, a doubtful case indeed, [is]
sometimes provided for by statute in motorin[g]
offences.[18]"

CONTENTS

OTHER BOOKS IN THE SERIES

TABLE OF CASES

TABLE OF STATUTES

Chapter 1

INTRODUCTION

1. *The Topic Defined*

This is a study of strict and vicarious liability from a functional perspective. It is desirable at the outset to be clear about terminology. By strict liability, I mean no more than that the prosecution need not prove *mens rea* as to some or all of the elements of the *actus reus* as part of its case in chief; in other words, it can secure a conviction without proving that the accused acted intentionally, recklessly or even negligently in respect of some or all elements of the *actus reus*. It is a generally held view that liability is best described as strict rather than absolute, the latter word quite wrongly suggests that there are no defences to crimes of strict liability.

Vicarious liability takes two forms. In one, a person is held liable for the acts of another who has *mens rea*. The context typically is that of the Licensing Acts. In the other, commoner case, a person is held liable for the act of another where the act of the other person amounts to an offence of strict liability. One example of the form is where a merchant is held liable for the sale of an article in circumstances which the law forbids, the actual physical act being that of his employee. Here the court recognises a nexus between employer and employee for the purposes of enforcement. Liability arises in both cases because the duty is cast upon the licensee or the employer: it may be regarded as vicarious, roughly speaking, because he is liable even though the employee was personally at fault and, conceivably, even if he was acting in breach of instructions.

The fact that the prosecution need not prove *mens rea* as to some or all elements of *actus reus* does not mean that no mental element is required in crimes of strict liability. There is a general principle that criminal liability requires at least that the accused have acted or omitted to act voluntarily.[1] This, while a general rule, may admit of exceptions. The most celebrated is *Rex* v. *Larsonneur*.[2] The accused was tried on indictment for being "found in" the United Kingdom, being an alien to whom leave to land was refused, contrary to immigration legislation then in force. The case was a particularly harsh one. Larsonneur, a French citizen, was given leave to land in the United Kingdom, but eight days later the conditions attached to her leave were varied and she was required to leave the United Kingdom. She then went to the Irish Free State whence she was deported in the custody of police, and brought to Holyhead. She was brought in British police custody from Holyhead to London for trial. The defence was that she did not voluntarily land. The jury found her guilty, "through circumstances beyond her control." According to the Lord Chief Justice, the circumstances of her going to Ireland were immaterial. When taken into custody in the United Kingdom, she was in the position of one who had been refused leave to land, and being found in the realm, was properly convicted of the offence. Clearly, the fact that she left the Irish Free State under compulsion and entered Britain under compulsion was not allowed to serve as a defence. It is not surprising that the decision has been referred to as the acme of injustice.[3]

Of *Rex* v. *Larsonneur* one must first ask what is its status as authority, and then to what statutory formulations it applies. It is, of course, not binding on the House of Lords. At least one attempt has been made to show that it must be understood in a more liberal sense than a literal reading of the judgement of the Court of Criminal Appeal would suggest. Professor Lanham suggests that while compulsion is a general defence to all crimes including those of strict liability, it did not apply in this case because the accused, by her voluntary acts, brought the compulsion on herself.[4] He argues that the accused was at fault, both in England by breaking the conditions of entry applicable to her, and in the Irish Free State as a result of which she was deported to England. The problems with this explanation are several in number. First, there seems no reason why the accused should not have been deported from the Irish Free State to France, her country of origin, if not directly, then through Britain in custody without being charged with an offence. Secondly, her misdeeds may have explained why the prosecution was brought, but they do not justify the verdict, for the jury, noting that she entered Britain under compulsion, seem to have wanted to mitigate her guilt thereby. Thirdly, the Lord Chief Justice at no time referred to fault on the accused's part as qualifying the scope of the decision; the court appears simply to have relied on the passive wording of the section. Professor Lanham's explanation of the case depends upon the unsound proposition that a harsh rule of law can be explained by reference to facts which the court could have taken into account even where there is no reason to suppose that it did so. If *Rex* v. *Larsonneur* is to be attacked, it will be necessary to do so directly.

There is, in fact, reason to think that *Rex* v. *Larsonneur* would not survive a challenge before the House of Lords, even though English and Commonwealth cases are not as clear as one could wish on the question whether a voluntary act or omission is required where the offence is expressed passively. In *Alphacell Ltd.* v. *Woodward*,[5] a case involving a charge of "causing" polluting matter to enter a river, their Lordships treat the case as one in which liability could be proven simply by proving the escape of pollutants from the company's installation; it was not necessary to show that any particular person actively caused pollutants to enter the water, or caused them to do so by failing to maintain filtration equipment. Their Lordships did not, however, indicate that no defences were available to a case of this character. Lord Wilberforce would have allowed a defence where pollution occurred as a result of an act of a third party, presumably a third party whose act was unforseeable and one against which reasonable precautions could not be taken.[6] Lord Pearson spoke of the absence of any intervening act of a trespasser, or of an act of God or freak weather conditions, intimating that these might serve as defences.[7] Lord Cross spoke of an event beyond the accused's control or foresight as possibly affording a defence,[8] and Lord Salmon, in the same vein, noted that there had been no active intervention of a stranger.[9] At least one distinguished Commonwealth judge has been prepared to infer from this that a total absence of fault may be a defence to even the most stringent of strict liability offences.[10]

Actual decisions on the question are unclear. In New Zealand, in *Kilbride* v. *Lake*[11] the court sought for a formulation which would excuse an accused where he neither acted nor omitted to act voluntarily. The appellant was charged under reg. 52(1) of the Traffic Regulations 1956, with operating a vehicle on which there was not displayed a current warrant of fitness. He had parked his car, which then displayed a current warrant of fitness, and on returning to it shortly thereafter, discovered that the warrant had disappeared and that there was a traffic offence notice on the windscreen. Woodhouse J. held that a person can only be made liable for an act or omission where it was done or omitted in circumstances, where there was no other course open to him. He thus states:[12]

> "If this condition is absent, an act or omission must be involuntary, or unconscious, or unrelated to the forbidden act in any causal sense regarded by the law as involving responsibility."

Here the infraction appeared to be attributable to the gratuitous act of a stranger; the accused had not done an act which the law forbade; he had not produced the prohibited event of the presence of the car combined with the absence of the warrant.

In *Strowger* v. *John*,[13] *Kilbride* v. *Lake* was distinguished on the facts. The accused was charged with failing to display a valid excise disc on his car windscreen. It had fallen from the windscreen. The court held that the accused must be convicted, but that the case might have been different had a third-party removed the disc, for in that case *Kilbride* v. *Lake* might have applied. This, with respect to a critical comment in the *Criminal Law Review*, seems to be correct, because the accused could, by careful inspection, have guarded against such an occurrence. The case is, therefore, not an authority for the proposition that no element of voluntariness is needed in strict liability offences, whether expressed in the active, or as here in the passive, voice.[14] There is at least one earlier case which suggests that it is no defence that a forbidden result was produced by the act of a stranger, but it is doubtful whether it is of much authority.[15]

It thus seems appropriate to conclude that crimes of strict liability require that the accused have acted or omitted to act voluntarily. M. Budd and A. Lynch sum the position up thus:[16]

> "An accused should not be convicted of any offence unless; (a) he had the physical opportunity and ability to act, or desist from acting, in order to prevent the crime; and (b) he knew [or ought to have known] that the prohibited harm would occur if he did not act, or desist from acting."

In addition there is widespread agreement among scholars that general defences such as duress, necessity, automatism and insanity apply to offences of strict liability.[17] Necessity indeed, is sometimes provided for by statute in motoring offences.[18]

Automatism must, of course, serve as a defence to crimes of strict liability, because it signifies that the accused neither acted nor omitted to do an act voluntarily.[19] Its application is discussed in chapter 4; it should be noted here, though, that vexed questions arise, especially in motoring cases, concerning how total incapacity must be before an act can be said to be involuntary. The question is what degree of incapacity to control events does the law require before involuntariness is made out?

Duress, necessity and insanity, again, afford defences to crimes of strict liability. A person is not held to be not guilty of crime where these defences apply because he lacked *mens rea* or *actus reus*. Some insane persons reason, and with peculiar intensity.[20] Both duress and necessity are based upon the proposition that in the particular case the accused had to make an invidious choice, and that his doing so was excusable under the circumstances. With due deference to the Law Commission which apparently thought otherwise, both in duress and necessity, courts balance the evils involved, though not always convincingly.[21] A person cannot simply take another's life to save his own, though he may be held not guilty where he acts as a secondary party only.[22] He may, however, be held to be justified in performing an abortion without going through the prescribed procedures, in a case where compliance is impracticable and a failure to perform the abortion would put the mother in imminent danger.[23] He may even, in some circumstances, be justified in escaping from gaol where to remain there would almost certainly result in his being harmed by others, whether inmates or guards.[24] In these cases, an overriding principle of non-responsibility applies to all offences, whether of strict liability or not. Indeed, it would be absurd, as well as contrary to principle, were duress to excuse a secondary party to murder, but not a person who sped through a Stop sign because he was compelled to do so.

There seems, then, ample reason to conclude that strict liability is seldom absolute, and that those cases which permit guilt in the absence of any element of voluntariness are unsound.

2. *The Importance of the Topic*

Why study strict and vicarious liability? On one level, at least, that of the construction of statutes, they have been the subject of much study. One obvious reason is that strict liability, and therefore most instances of vicarious liability, dispenses with *mens rea*, and permits the conviction of a person who, it is often argued, is either free from moral fault, or who has not been proved to be so at fault.[25] Should such an approach be tolerated, and if so within what limits? Another reason is the supposed novelty of the principles and their alleged inconsistency with existing doctrines of the criminal law. Both points are usually, and in my submission wrongly, taken as axiomatic. Yet another reason is the sheer inconsistency of doctrine which has resulted. Thus Professor Hogan writes that in England and Canada:[26]

> " . . . there is no discernible pattern even within the field of regulatory offences which enables the ordinary lawyer to predict with any measure of confidence whether a particular offence will be held to be one of strict liability or not. Few areas of the criminal law have spawned so much litigation and so little of it is edifying."

We are, he concludes, apt to meet social problems by creating crimes like confetti. Certainly there are few lawyers who would wish to argue that the cases on strict and vicarious liability present an orderly pattern; there is too much evidence that they do not.[27]

It is clear, on the other hand, that strict liability, vicarious liability and to some extent corporate criminal liability, are regarded as necessary elements in the enforcement of much modern legislation. The question is then seen as that of reconciling the exigencies of law enforcement with dictates of morality, and of bringing into harmony the principles of statutory construction which determine when an offence will be treated as one of strict liability and when it will not. These are the traditional preoccupations of lawyers.

In pursuing these preoccupations, honourable if trite, a number of issues, not always closely scrutinised, appear. For example, how true is it to say, of England and Wales at least, that offences are created indiscriminately, without, due regard to the interests of innocent persons who may be caught by the words of the statute? What defences are available? How are they structured, and why? When no set of defences appears in a statutory scheme, is this to be taken as a mere failure by governments to consider the implications of their actions? Are strict liability statutes administered with due regard to the desirability of prosecuting only in cases of fault? If the answer to this latter question is yes, then is the fault principle appropriate to some only, to most, or to all strict liability offences? Does vicarious liability have a place in the criminal law? If so, what purposes does it serve? What are the conditions for its imposition and are they defensible? How are strict and vicarious liability used today—what part do they play in enforcing regulatory schemes? All these and other questions require at least to be asked. It is misleading simply to stress the principles of statutory construction in considering these topics. Instead, one begins to look upon the criminal sanction from a functional perspective, viewing it as a necessary, but usually subordinate, adjunct to administrative schemes. The same comment applies to vicarious and to some extent to corporate liability, which require an enterprise to enforce regulatory legislation itself, securing adherence to it by its officers and employees. This is the emphasis with which this work approaches the topic. It does not ignore traditional preoccupations; it would be undesirable to do so, but it seeks to go beyond them.

3. *The Approach Taken*

The emphasis noted above will explain why this work does not treat the subject in quite the same way as certain distinguished predecessors. Its emphasis is on a functional perspective. While one must of course deal with the meaning given to words which appear often in the area of regulatory offences and which are said to attract or not to attract *mens rea*, words such as "causing" or "permitting", it would be misplaced zeal to attempt to emulate either professor J. Ll. J. Edwards' pioneering work or the later discussions of others.[28] Equally, it would not, I think, be helpful to venture yet another critique of the Model Penal Code, for that has been done by Professor Colin Howard.[29] Nor, I think, would it be right to stress as much as other writers have done, the alleged affront posed by strict liability to the need for the presence of moral fault as an essential condition of criminal guilt.[30] The reason for this is that much of the debate ignores what is a central preoccupation of this book, the presence in English law of affirmative defences which apply to a wide range of strict liability offences. For the same reason, it does not seem right to treat the possible evolution and adoption of a general no-negligence defence as a crucial issue, though it is clearly important and receives attention in these pages. It does not seem extravagant to suggest that some commentators berate the courts for not doing exactly that which Parliament has been astute to do. In this book, I have preferred to examine questions of morality after examining the facts, for there is little point in engaging in moralism on the basis of a false premise.

NOTES

[1] See *per* Lord Diplock in *Reg.* v. *Sheppard* [1981] A.C. 394 at p. 404F; J.C. Smith and B. Hogan, *Criminal Law* (4th ed. 1978), p. 79.

[2] (1933) 97 J.P. 206.

[3] Jerome Hall, "Interrelations of Criminal Law and Torts: II," 43 Col. L. Rev. 967 (1943) at p. 992 n.

[4] D. Lanham, "Larsonneur Revisited", [1976] Crim.L.R. 276.

[5] [1972] A.C. 824.

[6] *Ibid.* at p. 834.

⁷ *Ibid.* at p. 845.

⁸ *Ibid.* at pp. 846–847.

⁹ *Ibid.* at p. 847.

¹⁰ *Ministry of Transport* v. *Burnetts Motors Ltd.* [1980] 1 N.Z.L.R. 51 at p. 58 per Cooke J.; note, however, that in *Impress (Worcester) Ltd.* v. *Rees* [1971] 2 All E.R. 357, it was held that when pollution was attributable to the act of a stranger, it was not "caused" by the accused, so that the case could be decided on the relatively narrow ground of causation.

¹¹ [1962] N.Z.L.R. 590.

¹² *Ibid.* at p. 593.

¹³ [1974] Crim.L.R. 123.

¹⁴ The offence spoke of a person who kept a vehicle without there being fixed or exhibited a disc; see Vehicles (Excise) Act 1971, s.12.

¹⁵ *Parker* v. *Alder* [1899] 1 Q.B. 20.

¹⁶ M. Budd and A. Lynch, "Voluntariness, Causation and Strict Liability", [1978] Crim.L.R. 74.

¹⁷ M. Budd and A. Lynch, *supra*; I. Patient, "Some Remarks about the Element of Voluntariness in Offences of Strict Liability", [1968] Crim.L.R. 23; and see J. C. Smith and B. Hogan, *supra*.

¹⁸ *e.g.* Road Traffic Regulations Act 1967, s.79; further examples are contained in chapter 4.

¹⁹ In general, see H. L. A. Hart, "Acts of Will and Responsibility", in *Punishment and Responsibility* (1968), chapter 4.

²⁰ *e.g. Rex* v. *Hadfield* (1800) 27 St. Tr. 1281.

²¹ The Law Commission, *Report on Defences of General Application*, (Law Comm. No. 83, 1977), at paras. 4.28–4.33.

²² *Reg.* v. *Dudley and Stephens* [1881–5] All E.R. Rep 61; *Abbott* v. *R.* [1977] A.C. 755; *Lynch* v. *D.P.P. for N.I.* [1975] A.C. 653 in which Lord Simon declined to distinguish between duress and necessity.

²³ *e.g. see Morgentaler* v. *The Queen* [1976] 1 S.C.R. 616.

²⁴ *Reg.* v. *Loughnan* [1981] V.R.443.

²⁵ The point is argued most forcefully in Law Reform Commission of Canada, Working Paper No. 2, *Strict Liability* (1974).

²⁶ B. Hogan, "Working Paper 2 Strict Liability", (1975) 2 *Ottawa Law Review*, 258.

²⁷ *e.g.* J. Ll. J. Edwards, *Mens rea in Statutory Offences* (1955).

²⁸ J. Ll. Edwards, *Mens Rea in Statutory Offences* (1955).

²⁹ Colin Howard, *Strict Responsibility* (1963).

³⁰ P. Brett, *An Enquiry into Criminal Guilt*, esp. at pp. 121–123. These issues are further considered in chapter 6, *post.*

Chapter 2

THE EMERGENCE OF STRICT AND VICARIOUS LIABILITY

1. *The Common Law*

Strict liability and certainly vicarious liability are conventionally regarded as 19th century developments. The appearance of strict liability in two mid-nineteenth century cases has been treated as the abrupt dawn of a new body of doctrine, at variance with fundamental traditions of the common law.[1] In fact, this view appears to be both unhistorical and overstated. Nuisance was a strict liability crime from an early period.[2] It was the vehicle by which the hundred, and turnpike and canal companies were made liable for faults such as failures to repair roads and bridges.[3] While the common law indictment for nuisance was gradually superseded on the one hand by the equitable injunction and on the other by statutory offences under statutes like the Railway Clauses Consolidation Act, 1845, which created summary conviction offences for failure to maintain bridges, tracks and rights of way, its importance as an early measure of administrative control must be emphasised.

The 18th century statute book also affords harbingers of strict liability in the form of statutory defences to be proven by accused persons. Such provisions relate to the adulteration of tea, coffee and tobacco, and gave defences to merchants and others who could prove that such adulteration took place without their knowledge and despite their exercise of diligence to prevent it.[4] It would no doubt be unhistorical to argue that these reflect the acceptance of doctrines of strict liability from an early period. The modern rule concerning the burden of proof contained in *Woolmington's* case had not then been settled.[5] Today, the burden of proof lies upon the prosecution, and the only burden laid upon the accused is to collect from the evidence once the prosecution has raised a *prima facie* case against him, enough material to raise a reasonable doubt about his guilt for the jury. In the period before 1935 it was widely believed that in English law a killing, for example, was presumed to be murder unless the contrary appeared from circumstances of alleviation, excuse or justification, and this sort of burden was thought to apply to most offences.[6] If, today, a crime is cast in terms which do not explicitly mention a mental state, and a due diligence defence is created, it seems reasonable to assume that strict liability is intended subject to making out the excuse. In the 18th century, given the then attitude towards proof, it may have seemed to contemporary lawyers and courts that Parliament was simply engaged in specifying the particular matters which would have to be made out to displace the *prima facie* inference of guilt which would otherwise have been drawn from the sale of adulterated goods. In other words, such provisions may not have carried any implications for legal theory generally. What they probably show is that courts were inclined to view certain instances of adulteration or having adulterants in possession as sufficient to convict the defendant, and a legislative judgment that courts ought to find such persons liable unless the specific matters contained in the statutory defences were made out.

Indeed, the relative sophistication of the courts towards the statutory provisions in issue in the early cases can be gauged from the judgments themselves. In *Attorney-General v. Lockwood*,[7] a charge against a beer shop owner for having forbidden items in his possession, the court rejected the argument that, because it was possible to possess the articles innocently, it could not have been the intention of Parliament to convict a person without showing that his intention was wrongful. The answer to the argument that possible injustices might occur was that the Attorney-General, who alone could prosecute, would not do so in such instances. Four years later, when *Rex* v. *Woodrow* arose, the court noted that a defence of innocent possession had been provided by statute. In that case, dealing with adulterated tobacco, in which the Crown moved for forfeiture of the statutory penalty of £200, the court dealt with a series of issues that were obviously exercising people's minds at that time.[8] It noted, for example, the difficulty of proving guilt without strict liability, the power in the Commissioners of Customs and Excise to refrain from prosecution in a proper case, and the duty on the defendant, either to make proper inquiries concerning whether goods in his possession were adulterated, or to take a warranty that they were not from his supplier. As Parke B. stated:[9]

> "You must get some one to make that nice chemical analysis, or you must rely upon the manufacturer or dealer who sells to you, and take your remedy against him. You may take a warranty from him that it is lawful tobacco. There are very ample reasons for these provisions of the act, on account of the difficulty of convicting in such cases."

Similarly, Pollock C.B. saw nothing unreasonable in placing what amounts to an affirmative duty of care upon vendors, in matters affecting the revenue or the public health. Nor in such cases were the penalties necessarily pecuniary only. Under the Tea Act 1777, imprisonment could be imposed, while under the Tobacco Act of 1715, a vendor of adulterated tobacco could be fined, but the penalty provided for his guilty servant was imprisonment, a nice measure of economic discrimination, it would seem.

There thus seems some reason to think that strict liability can be traced to the 18th century, although it did not assume a developed form until a later period. It certainly arose before vicarious liability which had to await the growth of vicarious liability in tort. What its ambit was to be had to be determined, but there seems some reason to think that onus of proof provisions were not restricted to cases of pecuniary penalties only. If the thesis about its relation to the burden of proof is accepted, the introduction of the concept into some serious and traditional offences cannot seem wholly surprising. In some such offences, for example that of taking a girl under the statutory age from the custody of her father,[10] or receiving an insane person into unlicensed premises,[11] vexed problems of proof were bound to appear. It is no doubt possible to infer from the circumstances that a girl was living at home, that this was common knowledge and that an accused knew that he was taking her from the custody of her parents. It is much less safe to infer that a man knows the age of a girl, for she may well appear mature. Similarly, not every insane person is obviously so.

These, after all, were not the only instances in which extraordinary doctrines were introduced to cope with such problems. Under s.27 of the Theft Act 1968, which derives from s.19 of the prevention of Crime Act 1872, evidence of former instances of handling goods and of previous convictions for handling may be given in order to show that the accused knew that the goods which form the basis of a handling charge against him were stolen goods. Similarly, where an accused is found in possession of goods recently stolen, an inference may be raised against him either that he is the thief or a handler of them. It is true that this is said not to be a doctrine but only a common sense inference from the fact of possession.[12] That, with respect, seems rather to understate its force, for recent possession affords an inference in the common cases of receiving and handling that may go beyond the maximum inference that could otherwise be drawn from the mere fact of possession. Yet it does not permit inferences to be drawn that the accused obtained the goods by the means of any less common crime. It would certainly seem that where the evidence is as consistent with theft as with handling, the indictment should contain a count for each offence, albeit that the accused can be convicted of one only.[13] This is not the place to pursue that conundrum. It is enough to say that the courts and Parliament were commonly astute to devise doctrines to overcome evidentiary problems, and that strict liability should be seen in this light.

2. *The Extension of Strict Liability*

The further extension of strict and vicarious liability owed much to practical difficulties of enforcement; the inability otherwise to police efficiently the mass of regulatory legislation passed during the latter half of the nineteenth century. While, as we have intimated, public welfare legislation had been on the statute book for a considerable period, at no previous time had it been at all widespread or comprehensive in scope. During the nineteenth century, a great body of legislation was introduced, providing minutely for the regulation of various forms of activity. The Factory Act 1878, which replaced and consolidated much earlier legislation, is an example. It dealt with a wide range of matters relating to working conditions, and it was enforced by a corps of inspectors with broad powers to enter, inspect and examine factories, to require the production of certain documents, and to ensure that the provisions of the Act were being complied with. The Liquor Licensing Act 1872 regulated the sale of liquor and other practices on licensed premises. The Food and Drugs Act 1875 created offences in connection with the sale of food and drugs, the legislation to be enforced by medical officers of health, inspectors of weights and measures, inspectors of markets, and the police, in conjunction with the chemists, for the rise of chemical-analysis made impurities easier to detect. Other such legislation emerged as well. Legislation concerning public health was consolidated by the Public Health Act 1875. The Alkali Acts were consolidated in 1881. The Rivers Pollution Prevention Acts date from 1876 and 1893, and smoke nuisance was dealt with by a series of Acts including railway legislation of 1868[14] and the Public Health Act 1875.

No clear guidance as to the way in which the courts ought to interpret such legislation was given in it. The courts proceeded to deal with the resulting problems by a process of textual exegesis aided by a commonsense grasp of the public policy issues involved. We may take their approach to food and drugs legislation as an example.

Food and drugs and tobacco had often been adulterated convictions had been hard to secure, and increasingly severe legislation was adopted to deal with the problem. In the mid-nineteenth century, public awareness of adulteration became ever greater, partly as the result of the efforts of reforming doctors and *The Lancet*.[15] Pressure resulted in a series of enactments, dating from the Food and Drugs Act 1860. Enforcement was defective. Offences at first required *mens rea*, and were hard to prove, nor did administrative bodies capable of enforcing the legislation emerge overnight. Legislation was, however, progressively strengthened. Furthermore, the courts played a vigorous part in this. In three leading cases they held that no *mens rea* was required to convict persons of selling adulterated food as unadulterated contrary to section 2(2) of the Food and Drugs Act 1872.[16] This conclusion was based partly on the presence of the word "knowingly" in other provisions in the statute, and partly upon practical necessity. Advances in chemical analysis meant that the fact of adulteration could be more readily proven, but the rise in product standards made it more difficult to infer that a merchant knew that he was supplying goods which did not conform to standards. "Knowingly" was reserved for the actual offence of adulterating for which a penalty of imprisonment was provided under s.1 and for selling ingredients or material injurious to health, whether or not the seller knew them to be adulterated under s.2. Strict liability applied to the case where adulterated goods were sold as unadulterated, under s.2. Here, no word was used to denote mental state. Even though the penalty under both limbs of s.2 was the same, the contextual argument favoured strict liability.

Furthermore, a *mens rea* requirement would have rendered the provision ineffectual. But it is undeniable that the statute was obscurely drafted, the courts said as much, and the instances in which *mens rea* words were used in creating offences cannot, from the point of view of *practical* enforcement, always be differentiated from those in which they were not. No doubt the precise structure of the legislation owed a great deal to Parliamentary compromises which reflected a view that the stigma of acting so as to injure health should not apply to anyone who was not morally blameworthy.

Pragmatic realism can be seen in other 19th century cases, as well as in modern authorities.[17] Problems of enforcement, particularly in the ill-defined area of public welfare offences, explain its development, but explanation is not necessarily justification. In the first place, such liability extended, as we have noted, beyond the area of public welfare offences, into more serious crimes. Secondly, in respect of such offences, the imposition of strict liability seems not always to have been necessary. An example is the imposition of strict liability in respect of the status of a constable where the offence of assaulting a constable in the execution of his duty is concerned; there seems no reason why the prosecution should not, in a doubtful case, have been content with a charge either of common assault or, where serious injury was inflicted, one of the graver assault offences.[18] Thirdly, even in public welfare offences, the very strictness of liability which denied the relevance of due diligence was not shown to be necessary.[19] The courts obviously encountered difficulty in devising appropriate doctrines of interpretation to deal with expanding public welfare legislation. There was a tussle between the presumption of *mens rea*, asserted by some cases, and the demands of modern legislation to which it was said not to apply.[20] There was the question whether in the absence of *mens rea* words liability was strict, or whether the burden of proof was merely shifted, so that the defendant could defend himself by showing an absence of fault. This suggestion has since been definitively rejected, but it seemed a not unreasonable response to the problem of reconciling difficulties posed by the desirability of requiring fault on the one hand, and of securing the efficient enforcement of legislation on the other.[21] The notion of a due diligence defence to be proven by the accused has, as will be seen, been adopted in Australia.

3. *The Extension of Vicarious Liability*

The development of vicarious liability too, derived from problems of enforcement. Criminal libel and public nuisance apart, criminal liability had to be personal, not vicarious.[22] The court, however, chose to regard public nuisance as civil in substance, albeit criminal in form, and held that a master could be liable for his servant's conduct in creating a nuisance.[23] As Kenny put it:[24]

> "This special rule has the further justification that the master, by the very fact of setting a servant upon work that may result in a nuisance, has brought about a state of things which he ought at his peril to prevent from actually producing that result."

He was, indeed, made liable for conduct by the servant which he had actually forbidden.

The courts extended this liability to the liability of publicans for the acts and even the intent of their servants, to adulteration committed by a stranger, and the like. It extended even more readily to legislation which was construed as imposing strict liability. Such legislation was not regarded as creating crimes; instead, the courts held that offences contained in many modern statutes were less than criminal. They could be regarded as regulatory offences rather than crimes.[25] Because such offences were regarded as less than truly criminal, vicarious as well as strict liability could apply to them.

It is unnecessary to dwell unduly upon the earliest

cases, although they seem to show that the courts thought that without some such liability, enforcement of regulatory legislation would be difficult, if not impossible.[26] Policy considerations thus underlie the development of vicarious criminal liability; its shape was largely due to corresponding developments in the law of tort, and in particular in holding employers liable not upon some fiction of implied command, but upon the basis of employment, control and authority.[27] It seems clear enough that the burgeoning Victorian statute book created a plethora of new duties, all of which had to be enforced, some by Inspectorates, others by the police, and all hard-pressed.[28] If the master were permitted to escape because the fault was that of his servant, an easy excuse would have been created, and the master would not have been under the powerful incentive of liability to ensure enforcement of the legislation within the enterprise. There is no reason to doubt the justification for judicial fears concerning the enforcement of legislation.[29]

Subsidiary reasons for such liability can also be suggested. It would no doubt have been unjust to punish a mere servant for the act of sale of, for example, adulterated milk, when he lacked the means of detecting or preventing adulteration. Furthermore, even had he been aware of the facts constituting the offence, it might have meant his livelihood if he had failed to do the acts prohibited.[30]

Vicarious liability for *mens rea* offences rests in part upon the policy issues noted above and in part upon a further complication arising from the wording of particular statutes. The Licensing Act, 1872 for example, laid a statutory duty in express terms upon the licensee. Some sections apply to "any person" or "every one", but others apply to "every holder of a licence",[31] or to "any licensed person".[32] To permit a licensee to delegate management, and thus avoid personal knowledge of the commission of offences on his premises, would have removed those premises from the control scheme of the Act. The sort of problem which the courts faced is illustrated by *Redgate* v. *Haynes*.[33] Section 17 of the Licensing Act 1872 made it an offence for a licensed person to suffer gambling to be carried on in licensed premises. The licensee went to bed early and the hall porter drew his chair as far as possible from a private room in which three individuals were in fact gambling. The justices drew the inference that the hall porter removed his chair "to the greatest possible distance from that room . . . in order that he might not hear what passed there, and that such removal was directed by the appellant." Lord Blackburn held that the landlady could be liable whether she connived at gaming or whether, she no longer being on the premises, her servant connived at it. Here the justices could conclude that the porter suffered what was going on and went away that he might not hear. If knowledge on the part of the absent licensee were required, such a person could readily avoid conviction by absenting himself or herself from the premises.[34] The courts could, of course, have forced legislative change by strict construction of the provisions. They did not do so. Instead they applied a particularly sweeping form of vicarious liability to the problem.

The judgment of Lord Russell C.J. in *Commissioner of Police* v. *Cartman*,[35] a case arising under section 13 of the Licensing Act 1872, also illustrates this development very well. After indicating that in most cases licensees do not keep direct control over their businesses in their own hands, his Lordship concluded that for the Act to be enforced effectively, liability for the acts of his delegate had to be imposed on the licensee. But while this mode of thought was common in cases arising under the Licensing Acts, it was by no means exclusive to them. It applied commonly to cases where a person fitting a particular description was subjected to a statutory duty.[36] Such a person was apt to be made vicariously liable, whether for an offence of strict liability or for one involving *mens rea* on the footing that he could not be permitted to shuffle off his responsibilities by entrusting the actual conduct of his enterprise to another. Furthermore, *Chisholm* v. *Doulton*[37] illustrates that an employer might be made liable for the fault of a servant simply because it was assumed that the actual offender could not be located. Here liability had nothing to do with delegation or with a licence. It rested upon the language of the statute which imposed liability upon "the owner or master or other person having charge" of a vessel which unlawfully emitted smoke.

These instances of vicarious liability have been explained, wrongly it is submitted, on the basis that they are confined to public licensees and arise from the terms in which the licence is granted.[38] The true explanation was put most clearly by Halse Rogers J. in an Australian decision, *Alford* v. *Riley Newman Ltd.*, as follows:[39]

> "If the statute is one of the category of statutes regulating trade or business . . . and if also, a liability is thrown on the principal by terms expressly imposing the penalty on him, then he becomes responsible for the knowledge or intent of the servant—his *mens rea*. It is reasonable in such cases that the master on whom responsibility is placed should not be able to avoid that responsibility by putting in his place an agent who will have the *mens rea* which otherwise would be possessed by the master."

In the result, by the end of the 19th century, vicarious liability was recognised both for offences of strict liability and for some *mens rea* offences as well, though the latter had and have an anomalous character. The tests for liability also evolved during this period, and are dealt with in the next chapter.

The exigencies of enforcement were thus responsible for the evolution of strict and vicarious liability. In some instances this development was facilitated by the language in which courts were able to indulge. In many instances courts were, as we have seen, able to explain their abandonment of the *mens rea* principle and their imposition of vicarious liability as possible, because the infraction was not a true crime. This language was no doubt sometimes rhetorical, but it also corresponded to reality as many courts saw it.[40] Revenue infractions may well have seemed less than criminal. So too, no doubt, did some food and drug offences, even though malpractices in connection with these substances posed grave dangers to the public. The notion of quasi-criminal offences, or matters prohibited under a penalty, became and remained a staple of judicial thought.[41] The apotheosis of this mode of thought can be seen in the decision of Lord Haldane for the Privy Council in *Re Board of Commerce Act*[42] where, in construing a grant of power to the Parliament of Canada to legislate in relation to criminal law, his Lordship concluded that the power was only exercisable in relation to matters comprehended within a domain of criminal law bounded by notions of moral fault. This reasoning has since been rejected for the purposes of constitutional interpretation in Canada,[43] and stringently criticised by Professor Glanville Williams, on the basis that one cannot distinguish between crimes and mere infractions by reference to the supposed moral content of each.[44] To this question we return in the final chapter of this work.

The justification for strict and vicarious liability did not entirely depend on the notion that some matters were really not criminal. Courts rightly had regard to the severity of the penalty, imposing such liability in the public interest where it seemed necessary to do so, and where the injustice was at least mitigated by the notion that the penalty was pecuniary and often minor in character.[45] But, as we have indicated, some offences of partial strict liability at any rate, were not minor and could not, on any view, have been thought to be morally neutral. Here, as we have noted, the key was enforceability. Cases like *Bishop*[46] and *Prince*[47] posed, as we, have noted, problems of proof. It is noteworthy that both in the latter instance and in certain cases involving possession of narcotics, Parliament has in effect ratified the actual decision by creating defences for an accused which he must prove.[48] With due respect to more philosophical explanations, I should rather stress sheer pragmatism, concealed in many cases by a form of words chosen to permit the court to arrive at a construction of a penal provision which it judged necessary in the interests of enforcement as the key to development.[49]

In fastening upon problems of proof as the dominant impulse for the development of strict, and to a degree vicarious liability, I do not overlook other suggested explanations, such as that the number of petty cases would make it impossible for courts to investigate the intent of each accused, or that liability of an unqualified kind tends to force people to abide by regulatory legislation pertaining to their premises. But of the first of these, the fact is that most crimes are disposed of by a plea of guilty and this is likely to happen in any case where the prosecution is very likely to succeed. Thus viewed, it is an aspect of the problem of proof. The second argument would be persuasive only if no defences were in fact available, which is generally not the case. There seems no reason to think that people would abide by the law only if liability is both strict and absolute. Furthermore, today the question whether such liability could lead to greater care is a consideration in construing legislation as requiring the imposition of strict liability or not. The courts do not seem disposed to manipulate persons in this way, and the explanation is at best an unsatisfactory rationalisation after the event.[50] A further suggestion, that modern legislation is expressed more precisely than was once the case, and that therefore an absence of words usually understood as requiring *mens rea* indicates an intention to impose strict liability, is curiously unconvincing in the light of decisions on the meaning of words like causing, permitting, possession or even recklessness.[51] Language has not attained a sufficient certainty of meaning to enable us to consider that supposed justification to be very convincing.

It but remains to stress, again, that the application of the various canons of construction produced many inconsistencies. Why, for example, should *Prince* be an offence of partial strict liability while *Tolson*, a decision on bigamy, was construed as requiring *mens rea* as to the fact of being married, even though statutory defences were created for the accused, such as, for example, that the spouse had been continuously absent for seven years.[52] Admittedly, both the statutory defence and the *mens rea* principle can co-exist in that context. Nonetheless, the task of reconciliation has never been and perhaps cannot be successfully accomplished.

We may now turn to some aspects of the construction of legislation.

NOTES

[1] Colin Howard, *Strict Resposibility* (1963), p. 6.

[2] *Reg.* v. *Stephens* (1865) L.R. 1 Q.B. 702.

[3] On indicting the hundred, see. T.F.T. Plucknett, *Edward I and Criminal Law* (1960) p. 89; for authorities on vicarious liability, nuisance and criminal libel, see L. H. Leigh, *The Criminal Liability of Corporations in English Law* (1969) ch. 2.

[4] See for example, Bread Act 1773, s.6; Bread Act 1836, s.13; Tea Act 1774, s.4; by contrast some earlier statutes such as the Customs Act 1720, c. 11, speak of knowingly adulterating coffee and tea, and there are other examples in the 18th century statute book.

[5] [1935] A.C. 462.

[6] See *Jayasena* v. *The Queen* [1970] A.C. 618 at p. 623 *per* Lord Devlin.

[7] (1842) 9 M. & W. 378.

[8] (1846) 15 M. & W. 404.

[9] *Ibid.*, at p. 413.

[10] *Reg.* v. *Prince* (1875) 2 C.C.R. 154; note that the particular enforcement problem is overcome today by the creation of a special defence; see Sexual Offences Act 1956, s.19.

[11] *Reg.* v. *Bishop* (1879) 5 Q.B.D. 259.

[12] *D.P.P.* v. *Nieser* [1959] 1 Q.B. 254.

[13] *Reg.* v. *Seymour* [1954] 1 All E.R. 1006.

[14] Railways Clauses Consolidation Act, 1845, s.114 as amended by regulation of Railways Act, 1868, s.19.

[15] I. Paulus, *The Search for Pure Food: A Sociology of Legislation in Britain* (1974); "Strict Liability: Its place in Public Welfare Offences" (1978) 20 Cr.L.Q. 445.

[16] *Fitzpatrick* v. *Kelly* (1873) L.R. 8 Q.B. 337; *Roberts* v. *Egerton* (1874) L.R. 9 Q.B. 494; *Blaker* v. *Tillstone* [1894] 1 Q.B. 345.

[17] *e.g. Bruhn* v. *The King* [1909] A.C. 317 (P.C.).

[18] *Reg.* v. *Maxwell and Clanchy* (1909) 2 Cr.App.R. 26; *Albert* v. *Lavin* (1981) 72 Cr.App.R., at p. 183, affirmed on other grounds, *The Times*, December 4, 1981; and see C. Howard, "Assaulting Policemen in the Execution of Their Duty", (1963) 79 *L.Q.R.* 247.

[19] *Parker* v. *Alder* [1899] 1 Q.B. 20, stringently criticised by J. Ll. J. Edwards, *Mens Rea in Statutory Offences* (1955) at pp. 236–38.

[20] *Hobbs* v. *Winchester Corporation* [1910] 1 K.B. 471.

[21] *e.g.* compare *Hearne* v. *Garton* (1859) 28 L.J.M.C. 216, and *Core* v. *James* (1871) L.R. 7 Q.B. 135 with *Hobbs* v. *Winchester Corporation* (above), and *Reg.* v. *St. Margaret's Trusts Ltd.* [1958] 1 W.L.R. 522.

[22] *Rex* v. *Huggins* (1730) 2 Ld. Raym. 1574.

[23] *Reg.* v. *Stephens* (1866) L.R. 1 Q.B. 702.

[24] C.S. Kenny, *Outlines of Criminal Law* (1902) at p. 46.

[25] *e.g. Provincial Motor Cab Co.* v. *Dunning* [1909] 2 K.B. 599 at p. 602; there are many other examples.

[26] *Rex* v. *Dixon* (1814) 3 M. & S. 72; *A.G.* v. *Siddon* (1830) 1 Cr. & J. 220.

[27] The development is traced by Baty, *Vicarious Liability* (1916); see also F. James, "Vicarious Liability", 28 *Tulane L. Rev.* 161.

[28] On problems of enforcement under the Factories Acts, see W. Carson, "The Institutionalization of Ambiguity: Early British Factory Acts", in G. Geis and E. Stotland (eds.), *White Collar Crime: Theory and Research*, 142–173 (1980).

[29] *Collman* v. *Mills* [1897] 1 Q.B. 396; *Coppen* v. *Moore (No.2)* [1898] 2 Q.B. 306.

[30] See "Corporations as Criminals" (1924) 88 *J.P.* 198.

[31] Liquor Licensing Act 1875, s.7 (sale of spirits to children).

[32] *Ibid.*, s.10 (illicit storing of liquor); s.13 (permitting drunkenness); s.14 (keeping disorderly house); s.15 (permitting premises to be used as a brothel); s.16 (harbouring constable or supplying liquor to a constable on duty) ; s.17 (permitting gaming) ; s.20 (possession of adulterated liquor).

[33] (1876) 1 Q.B.D. 89.

[34] See further, C.S. Kenny, *op. cit.* at p. 47.

[35] [1896] 1 Q.B. 855; and see *Emary* v. *Nolloth* [1903] 2 K.B. 264.

[36] *Redgate* v. *Haynes* (1876) 1 Q.B.D. 89; *Allen* v. *Whitehead* [1930] 1 K.B. 211; *Linnett* v. *Commissioner of Metropolitan Police* [1946] K.B.

290; *Crabtree* v. *Fern Spinning Co. Ltd.* (1902) 85 L.T. 549; *Department of Agriculture* v. *Burke* [1915] 2 Ir. R. 128.

[37] (1889) 22 Q.B.D. 736.

[38] G.L. Williams, *Criminal Law, The General Part* (2 ed. 1961), p. 272. Support for this view comes also from *Massey* v. *Morris* [1894] 2 Q.B. 412.

[39] (1934) 34 S.R. (N.S.W.) 261 at p. 273.

[40] *cf.* G.L. Williams, "The Definition of Crime", [1955] C.L.P. 107 at p. 118; I agree that such infractions are crimes, but not that courts always used the expressions as a mere verbal device for treating such conduct as crime.

[41] *e.g.*, *Davis* v. *Harvey* (1879) L.R. 9 Q.B. 433 at p. 440 *per* Blackburn J.; *Collman* v. *Mills* [1897] 1 Q.B. 396; the matter is discussed at length by Sayre, "Public Welfare Offences", 33 Col. L. Rev. 55 (1933).

[42] [1922] 1 A.C. 191 at pp. 198–199.

[43] *Proprietary Articles Trade Association* v. *A.G. for Canada* [1931] A.C. 310 at p. 324.

[44] G.L. Williams, "The Definition of Crime" [1955] C.L.P. 107.

[45] R.M. Jackson, "Absolute Prohibition in Statutory Offences", (1938) 6 C.L.J. 83, and see *Laird* v. *Dobell* [1906] 1 K.B. 131; *Srinivas* v. *King-Emperor*, I.L.R. 1947 Patna 460 (P.C.).

[46] (1880) 5 Q.B.D. 259.

[47] (1875) L.R. 2 C.C.R. 154.

[48] Sexual Offences Act 1956, s. 19.

[49] *cf.* F.G. Jacobs, *Criminal Responsibility* (1971) , p. 109.

[50] These points, and others are fully discussed in C. Howard, *Strict Responsibility* (1963), pp. 9–28.

[51] *Kenny's Outlines of Criminal Law* (18th ed., Turner, 1962), p. 42, a suggestion deriving from Stephen J. in *Cundy* v. *Le Coq.* (1884) 13 Q.B.D. 207.

[52] (1889) 23 Q.B.D. 168; note that, by contrast to many defences in strict liability offences, the burden of proof is always on the prosecution in bigamy; if evidence appears from which it may be inferred that the deceased had not been seen during the seven years last passed, the prosecution must prove that the missing spouse was alive during that time. *Reg.* v. *Lind* (1921) 16 Cr.App.R. 31; *Reg.* v. *Peake* (1922) 17 Cr.App.R. 22.

Chapter 3

SOME ASPECTS OF CONSTRUCTION

1. *The Ambit of Strict Liability*

The problems which arise in construing statutory offences as involving strict or vicarious liability are admirably dealt with in the standard textbooks, and I do not propose to rehearse all of them in detail here. My interest is simply to indicate in respect of what matters strict liability will generally be imposed, then to discuss some of those exceptional cases in which serious crimes are construed as crimes of strict liability, and finally to draw attention, briefly, to some of the inconsistencies which result from interpretations which apparently fasten upon the supposed meaning of words divorced from the context in which they are used.

In construing statutory offences, there is a presumption favouring *mens rea*. Cases asserting the contrary have now been discredited.[1] This, as we have noted, has not prevented the courts from treating quite serious offences as offences wholly or partly of strict liability. It suffices to note that offences of unlawful possession of a firearm,[2] of an undischarged bankrupt obtaining credit,[3] and of assault upon a police officer,[4] fall within this category. Nonetheless, Wright J. in *Sherras* v. *de Rutzen* [1895] 1 Q.B. 918 identified three classes of case in which strict liability is most likely to be imposed:[5]

(a) acts which are not criminal in the real sense, but are prohibited in the public interest under a penalty;

(b) public nuisances; and

(c) cases in which, although the procedure is criminal in form, it is really only a summary mode of enforcing a civil right.

The first category, which is the one with which we are principally concerned, is obviously protean. Jerome Hall, aware of the diversity of offences which attract strict liability, nonetheless offered the following useful generalization.[6]

"First, many of the enactments apply not to the general public but only to certain traders, particularly to suppliers of food or drugs and vendors of alcoholic beverages. Others, having more general application as to potential offenders, are restricted to very few activities—the operation of automobiles, safety of highways, hunting, fishing, and various health measures. Next, many of these regulations and the conditions of conforming to them presuppose a continuous activity, such as carrying on a business. This implies that general standards regarding such conduct are important rather than isolated acts. Third, the public welfare enactments are relatively new. They represent relatively recent adaptations to an intricate economy, including an impersonal market . . . Thus, fourth, the modern regulations are not strongly supported by the mores."

Hall's remarks are, of course, generalisations only. The rough image which they evoke does not catch all the cases of strict liability which are recognised at any one time, nor does it tell us what offences may come to be regarded either as serious or venial. Nor do the words of Wright J. in *Sherras* v. *de Rutzen* carry us very far, because they express a conclusion rather than the reasons for it. Views of what is criminal in the real sense are obviously contingent upon public morality which is apt to change over time. It would, for example, be difficult to deny that oil pollution is now regarded by many persons as criminal. People may well, however, hold very different views of

The rationale of strict liability, and of vicarious and to some extent corporate liability as well, is that it causes employers to police their enterprises, ensuring that legislative standards are maintained within them. In a leading Canadian decision, *Reg. ex rel Carswell* v. *City of Sault St. Marie*,[15] Dickson J. indeed goes so far as to say that although enforced as penal law through the utilisation of the machinery of the criminal law, regulatory or public welfare or strict liability offences are civil in substance and might well be regarded as a branch of administrative law, to which traditional principles of criminal law have only limited application.

We are, therefore, if not exclusively in the realm of offences pertaining to enterprise liability (for road traffic offences for example affect everyone), or minor offences (for some crimes of pollution for example attract heavy penalties), at least frequently dealing with offences which govern enterprises from any of a number of aspects, including most prominently public health, safety and consumer protection. But the question naturally arises what the limits of liability are to be, for those three categories justify legislation which, potentially at least, affects a wide range of human conduct. Many traditional crimes plainly concern them; manslaughter concerns acts which pose a risk to human life; criminal deception covers part of the field of consumer protection; legislation concerning the administration of a noxious substance affects public health.

In order to restrict the potential ambit of strict liability, the courts have fashioned a limiting principle; not only must they inquire whether the activity concerned poses a grave social evil, but also whether strict liability will assist in the enforcement of the law. The court must, accordingly, ask whether there is something which the accused can do, directly or indirectly, by supervision or inspection or improvement of business methods or by exhorting those whom he can control, to promote observance of the legislation. If not, there is no reason to penalise him,

" . . . and it cannot be inferred that the legislature imposed strict liability merely to find a luckless victim".[16] This principle clearly comprehends cases of practical impossibility of compliance, as where the facts constituting the offence could not be known either to the accused, or to persons in his general situation, who could not, accordingly, do anything to promote the observance of the legislation.[17]

Three points should, however, be noted about this limitation. The first is that it addresses the generality of cases and asks whether the accused in a typical situation at which the prohibition is directed, could not, in common with others so circumstanced, have done anything to promote observance of the law. The second repeats a point mentioned earlier, namely, that strict liability is not imposed simply because the legislator deals with a grave social evil, for that would risk the wholesale extension of strict liability.[18] The third is that the case must, surely, be one in which strict liability is necessary in order properly to enforce the law, as for example where proof would otherwise be difficult to secure, since otherwise the limiting principle would instead be appropriate to expand the ambit of strict liability. Indeed, the question whether an offence could otherwise be proved underlies, as we have seen, both strict and vicarious liability and may again be looked upon both as a principle justifying such liability and as a limitation to it in cases where proof of the elements of the offence can be made without undue difficulty.[19]

In the final analysis, we deal with questions of public policy to which conventional principles of construction and even the presence of what might be considered *mens rea* words are subordinate.[20] It is this aspect of the topic which causes most difficulty, for the results of statutory interpretation are difficult to predict.

2. *Possession Offences and Strict Liability*

A striking example of the subordination of concepts to the dictates of public policy concerns the concept of possession. Whether possession has a standard or preferred meaning in which a possessor must know both that he has a thing, and that it has particular attributes, is a question which need not be argued here. The point is that the courts have attributed different meanings to the concept, and have been guided by the dictates of public policy in so doing. The problem goes back at least as far as *Reg.* v. *Ashwell*[21] where the Court for Crown Cases Reserved divided on the question whether, in the law of larceny, a man could be said to possess a sovereign when he thought that he had a shilling. It was held that he did not. In *Chajutin* v. *Whitehead*, however, where the offence was of possessing an altered passport, Lord Hewart C.J. considering that the legislation would be ineffectual if it were necessary to prove knowledge of the alterations, held that the defendant need only intend to possess the thing without knowledge of its attributes.[22]

The leading modern case is *Reg.* v. *Warner*.[23] The question of defences in respect of innocent possession has since been dealt with by statute. The decision remains of interest on the question of possession. The appellant picked up two boxes from a cafe proprietor. When he was stopped by the police, one was found to contain scent, and the other 20,000 tablets of amphetamine sulphate, a controlled drug under the Drugs (Prevention of Misuse) Act 1964. He was charged with the unauthorised possession of a scheduled drug, contrary to s.1(1) of the Drugs (Prevention of Misuse) Act 1964. The appellant contended that he though that both boxes contained scent. The jury was directed that lack of knowledge of the contents of the box went only to mitigation, and convicted him. On ultimate appeal to the House of Lords, it was held that the jury had been misdirected, but the conviction was upheld under the proviso.[24] On the question of the meaning of possession, a lively debate ensued.

Their Lordships agreed that mere physical control of an object without any mental element, cannot constitute possession. Lords Pearce and Wilberforce, with whom

Lord Reid concurred on the point, were prepared to hold that a person possesses a prohibited drug where he knows that he has a drug in his possession, albeit he does not know that the drug falls within a category which is prohibited. To require greater knowledge would, it is said, impair enforcement of the Act since many pedlars would be unaware of the precise nature of the drug. In their Lordships' view, a person would thus be in possession of drugs unless he believed, perhaps because he had been given a sealed packet, that the contents were quite different in kind. This would not leave that individual entirely without means of protection, but it is noticeable that "possession" is being made the support for a good deal of social engineering, for the concept as thus defined is made to produce this result:[25]

> "Thus the *prima facie* assumption [that he was in possession of the contents] is discharged if he proved (or raises a real doubt in the matter) either (*a*) that he was a servant or bailee who had no right to open it *and* no reason to suspect that its contents were illicit or were drugs or (*b*) that although he was the owner he had no knowledge of (including a genuine mistake as to) its actual contents or their illicit nature and that he received them innocently and also that he had no reasonable opportunity since receiving the package of acquainting himself with its actual contents."

It is at least surprising to have read into the concept of possession either that a mere servant who asserts no property in goods possesses them unless he had no reason to suspect the contents of the package in which they were contained, or that an innocent owner possesses illicit drugs if he knows that a packet contains drugs which he thinks to be innocent, but fails to verify this. If knowledge of the contents of a package is relevant to the question whether one possesses it, it is hard to see why a person who thinks that a packet containing drugs contains scent does not possess the drug, while a person who thinks that it contains drugs which he may lawfully have, for example aspirin, possesses prohibited drugs if he puts the packet, unopened, into his medicine chest. It is presumably these incongruities which led Lord Morris to insist on full knowledge, and Lord Guest to opt for the other polar extreme of treating the offence as absolute in the sense that the only mental element required is knowledge of the container, while recognising that possession, in some contexts and for some purposes, could require full knowledge of the attributes of the thing possessed. This latter mode of thought may explain *Hussain*[26] in which the accused was convicted of the unlawful possession of a firearm contrary to s.1 of the Firearms Act 1968 even though he apparently believed it to be a mere toy. The offence, the court holds, is absolute; the prosecution need not show that he knew of the nature of the article. Presumably, the dangers associated with firearms explain why a strict view was taken against the accused. As the *Criminal Law Review* points out, he must surely at least know of the presence of the article in his house or on his person.

Another example of the variant meanings of possession occurs in *Reg.* v. *Pierce Fisheries Ltd.*, a decision of the Supreme Court of Canada.[27] That court had previously insisted upon full knowledge of the attributes of the thing possessed, but that was in relation to possession of narcotics for which a substantial penalty of imprisonment was imposed.[28] *Pierce Fisheries Ltd.* concerned an offence of possession of under-sized lobsters, contrary to Fisheries legislation. A few under-sized lobsters were found on the defendant's premises. A majority of the court held that possession in this context only requires that the possessor have knowledge of the presence of the thing or things, but not necessarily of all its attributes, as here, its size. The presumption in favour of a requirement of full knowledge is thus apt to be displaced by the context. While textual considerations played a part in the court's decision—a narrow category of defences had been provided—the

dominant considerations were first that effective enforcement was necessary in the interests of conservation and
strict liability was required for it, and secondly that the
defendants could stimulate their employees to check
catches which the company purchased, thereby promoting
observance of the legislation.

Reasoning like this obviously enables the courts to give
very different meanings to possession, depending on the
context. It is this which the courts regard as justifying a
decision not to require knowledge of all the attributes of a
thing possessed and, indeed, to select those, all or any,
knowledge of which may be dispensed with.

3. *Some Inconsistencies in the Construction of Mens Rea Words*: *Permitting, Causing, Uses*

Similar inconsistencies in treatment apply to other words.
This is particularly true of such words as "permitting" and
"causing."[29] "Permitting" has been said, by Lord Diplock, to be a classic *mens rea* word; one cannot permit
that of which one lacks knowledge; and this is generally
how it is treated.[30] Indeed, "knowingly permits" is said to
add nothing to "permits". Actual knowledge is
required.[31]

Glanville Williams concluded, rather gloomily, that
" . . . it seems impossible in this part of the law to state
any plain and simple rule without having to set out
decisions in which it has been ignored."[32] There are
conflicting lines of authority on the word. One line, many
but not all of the cases on which deal with permitting use
of a defective vehicle, requires full *mens rea* for permitting
use in contravention of the relevant road traffic
legislation.[33] Another, dealing with permitting use of a
vehicle while uninsured, requires only an intent to permit
the vehicle to be used; the prosecution need not show
either that the defendant intended to permit the vehicle to
be used while uninsured, or that he was wilfully blind to
the possibility of such use.[34] Similarly, where a charge of

permitting an unlicensed person to drive a motor vehicle is concerned, the courts have held that the defendant need only have intended to permit use of the vehicle; honest mistake whether the driver was licensed is no defence.[35] But, while mistake is no defence, the defendant may safely permit use on the condition that the vehicle is properly insured, in which case the defendant cannot be held liable if it is not. A permission granted subject to a condition which is not complied with, is no permission at all.[36]

The courts have been content to note the different connotations of "permits" with no attempt at explanation at all. They have simply asked whether a given case is more closely analogous to the defective vehicle cases, or the "use without insurance" cases. It is evident that in some, but not all situations, they divine the legislative purpose as that of requiring the defendant either to take care that the law is complied with or else, by granting permission subject to a condition, to shift the burden of compliance with the penal provision on to another. That is true of the insurance cases, and it is also true of cases where, by imposing a duty of supervision upon employers, their employees can be stimulated to comply with the legislation, for example the regulations governing hours of work. In the latter case, "permits" was held to incriminate not only an employer who shuts his eyes to the obvious, but also one who failed to take adequate steps to ensure that his instructions were complied with.[37]

It is difficult to suggest a rational explanation of the authorities, either by invoking textual considerations, or by reference to the dictates of public policy. The provision considered in most of these cases, s.201 of the Road Traffic Act 1960, simply says that it shall be an offence for a person to use, or to cause or permit any other person to use a motor vehicle on a road unless use of the vehicle by the owner or driver is covered by a valid policy of insurance. The present state of the authorities cannot convincingly be explained on the footing that in some instances the public interest requires partial strict liability, while in others full *mens rea* is required. The problem with any such explanation is that it is very difficult indeed to see why the public interest should require full *mens rea* in the vehicle maintenance cases, but not in the insurance cases. One would have thought the arguments to be of equal weight in either case. Another explanation is perhaps that the divergent lines of authority are simply accepted by the courts on the basis of their antiquity, pending review by the House of Lords. Yet another, more mundane suggestion, is that counsel have simply failed to bring to the attention of the Divisional Court comments in the House of Lords concerning "permitting" which might have sufficed to tip the balance.

The essential consideration must surely be that the law be tight enough to ensure that persons in a position to control the use of vehicles by others will not permit their use by unlicensed or uninsured persons, or while such vehicles are in a dangerous state mechanically. It is right that such persons should be placed under strict duties to ensure that unlawful use will not occur. There seems little reason why permitting, in these contexts, should not generally be an offence of strict liability. Strict liability is, after all, adopted in order to make it difficult for a person upon whom a statutory duty is imposed to shuffle it off on another. The insurance cases in particular impose control at two pressure points, that of the controller and that of the user, rather than the latter alone, and impose strict liability upon both controller and user.

"Causes" is another word much used in statutes, in particular those dealing with road traffic. Once again, it sometimes implies strict liability, but there are instances when it is said to be inconsistent with strict liability. Thus, in *Alphacell Ltd.* v. *Woodward*[38] causing polluting matter to enter a river was held to be a strict liability offence, a result reached partly because other offences under the statute were cast in terms of "knowingly permits". A similar result was reached in a decision dealing with causing the use of a vehicle as an express carriage otherwise than under a road service licence, although there the decision seems also to rely on the consideration that the defendant could have made inquiries or have advised the company whose workers it was carrying of the requirements of the law.[39] Again, no *mens rea* was required on a charge of causing a stage play to be presented before the permission of the Lord Chamberlain had been procured.[40] Examples could be multiplied, but it seems sufficient to note that often "causes" is taken to raise the issue whether there was causation, but not whether *mens rea* was present.[41]

On the other hand, the authorities hold that a person cannot be held liable for causing user of a vehicle in contravention of the construction and use regulations unless he gives some express or positive mandate to the actual user with knowledge that such use will be in contravention of the regulations.[42] But a licensee whose servant sold a short measure of whisky to a customer contrary to s.24(1) of the Weights and Measures Act 1963 was held to have caused the sale, notwithstanding his ignorance of it. He was made strictly liable for the actions of his employee.[43]

Where the compound phrase "uses a vehicle or causes or permits it to be used" is used, as it is under the Motor Vehicle (Construction and Use) Regulations, the question whether the defendant is convicted or not may depend not upon the nature of his conduct, but upon whether he is charged with "permitting" user, rather than use itself. The courts have criticised this result as incongruous, but it is well established.[44] English cases proceed upon the premise that both an employer and his employee may use a vehicle in contravention of the legislation. An employer could well permit or cause use by an employee. Any person or firm having control of a vehicle can permit use by another. Thus, for example, a firm which let vehicles on hire could commit the offence of permitting user in contravention, seemingly, it could also cause such use, but

it would not itself use the vehicle, at any rate on a
highway. Here, one encounters a problem in the dual
meaning of words. An employer is considered to use a
vehicle when his employee uses it on his business, but a
vehicle lessor does not use a vehicle which is being driven
by the person to whom he leases it because the absence of
a master-servant relationship means that there is no nexus
between the lessor and the actual user such that the actual
use may be imputed to the lessor.[45] The result of any given
case may thus depend upon the choice of charge.
Australian courts adopt a different construction, holding
that an employer alone uses a vehicle on the highway, and
not the servant. A servant drives the vehicle, a narrower
concept. In the result, the statutory duty and the
prohibition lie upon the person undertaking the activity. It
would seem to follow that simple user is an offence
directed primarily at the undertaker, while permitting and
causing, though often applicable to him, were included
because of their wider application against others.[46] The
relevance of all this is that the courts have had to
determine what coverage it was intended that the law
should have. If *mens rea* were required throughout, the
law would have a narrow reach. By interpreting the
legislation more widely English courts, made the actual
user of a vehicle a virtual insurer of its safety while
Australian courts exempted the driver but held his
employer liable, perhaps an unwise concession. *Mens rea*
is reserved for one who permits or causes actual user by
another. In the result, there is no real gap in enforcement:
someone will be liable for the use of a defective vehicle.

4. *Omissions to Act*

A particular problem of this genre concerns omissions to
act. In *Harding* v. *Price*[47] Lord Goddard C.J. held that a
person could not be convicted of failing to give notice of
an accident unless it could be shown that he was aware of
the event, the accident, which placed him under a duty to

report it. The point is that the duty arises on the occurrence of the event, and the Lord Chief Justice could not see how failure to perform such a duty could properly lead to a conviction unless the person concerned were aware of the event upon which it is predicated.

It cannot be said that this decision has always been followed. It is not entirely consistent with earlier authority.[48] Indeed, the distinction between cases of omission and commission has been said, on high authority, to be insubstantial.[49] Modern cases are in conflict. In *Atkinson* v. *Sir Alfred McAlpine & Son Ltd.*,[50] the firm was held liable, *inter alia*, for failing to notify to the proper authority within the time limited, that it was to undertake in a factory a process involving blue asbestos. Its defence was that it neither knew, nor could reasonably be expected to have known, of the presence of blue asbestos. This notwithstanding, the court held that the offence was absolute, so strict a holding being required on grounds of public policy. On the other hand, in *Reg.* v. *Miller*,[51] James L.J., in a dictum, treated Lord Goddard's formulation as of general application; in such a case an accused should, his Lordship states, "be able to place before a jury his state of mind as to whether the event had in fact arisen on which the positive act was required to be performed."

It is probable that there is no special rule applicable to omissions. In some instances awareness of the event giving rise to the duty will be required; in others it will not. As always, public policy considerations can be prayed in aid of either construction and the result cannot readily be predicted. It is certainly difficult in most cases to see how the imposition of liability in the absence of awareness of the circumstances imposing the duty can be said to assist in the enforcement of the law, but the same may be said of cases where an obligation is breached by doing a prohibited act. In both instances, the nub of the defendant's complaint is that he was not aware of the facts and circumstances upon which liability is based. Consequently, one is driven back to the considerations outlined in

Lim Chin Aik and other cases, namely, whether by imposing liability one can induce a person to take greater care concerning how he conducts his trade or business, or activities. Viewed thus, a defensible distinction can be suggested between cases of failing to report an accident, and cases of failing to report an intention to engage in activity requiring the removal, for example, of blue asbestos. There, a strict liability offence may well concentrate the mind of the undertaker. The fault lies not in imposing strict liability; that is, in enabling the prosecution to succeed without proving that the firm was aware of the presence of blue asbestos; but in failing to provide a positive defence for a firm which took all reasonable care to comply with the regulations by inquiring into the presence of the prohibited substance or, alternatively, in bringing a prosecution which appears to be unmeritorious.

The inconsistencies noted above are not simply of interest as demonstrating that courts interpret the same word inconsistently from offence to offence. They also demonstrate that courts are inconsistent in the view which they take of whether broad questions of public policy ought to be considered in relation to statutory interpretation. Public policy considerations clearly underly judicial approaches to pollution legislation: *Alphacell* v. *Woodward* is a clear indication of this. The cases dealing with permitting the use of vehicles in contravention of the construction and use regulation on the one hand and insurance legislation on the other suggests either that courts have endeavoured to interpret the legislation by reference to textual considerations alone, or have for some unexplained reason, taken different views of the public policy involved in either context. Policy views clearly underly *Sopp* v. *Long* [1970] 1 Q.B. 518 on the obligation of licensees for sales made by their servants, but can they be said to underly cases on causing user of vehicle in contravention of construction and use regulations? The point is simply that unless courts articulate their reasons of policy for interpreting the same word or phrase differently, confusion is bound to result, unless indeed, the statutory context in which the words are found makes the matter plain.

Whether ultimately, *mens rea* is or is not dispensed with, either wholly or as respects some aspects of *actus reus*, often depends more upon judicial views of public policy, of what enforcement of a statutory scheme really requires, than upon purely lexical considerations. This point is evident in what has already been said concerning the vicarious liability of licensees. None of this is to say that the language in which statutes create offences alone never affords assistance in construction, for plainly it does. The point is, however, that tacit and conflicting judicial views of whether and the way and extent to which questions of public policy may be invoked in interpretation permeate this entire area and that they give rise to contradictory lines of authority. In the result these are often difficult to reconcile and so the same words are given different meanings under different statutory schemes, even though the nature of the enforcement problem is little different in either case.

There is a further point in all this. Confusion appears to be most prevalent in those cases where the statute is least explicit. In many areas, statutes which create offences also specify what defences will be available to an accused. This, as will be seen, is true of offences concerning food and drugs. By specifying defences, the legislation enables the court to take an informed view of what the affirmative bases of liability ought to be. Where the court can only rely on the words which create the offence, confusion is almost inevitable. Words can have more than one meaning. "Recklessly", for example, can refer to a mental state, or it may function as an adverb of manner only.[52] "Causing", or "permitting" may be construed with or without reference to mental state. We have referred to administrative criminal law: problems of interpretation most readily arise when the full conditions of liability are not worked out in any given scheme, and a failure to work out such conditions may either reflect that the need to do more than create offences was not foreseen, or that the words used were thought to have a more certain meaning than they were later given, or that no one thought that a *mens rea* requirement would ever be insisted upon. Certainly, most vexed questions of interpretation have arisen in those areas where both the wording of offences and the provisions of conditions of exculpation have not been carefully addressed by the legislature.

5. *Vicarious Liability*[53]

Similar problems arise, again, in connection with vicarious liability, where courts experience difficulties in determining to which offences it applies. Once again, the question whether such liability is necessary in the enforcement of public welfare legislation predominates. It has always been the case that offences under such statutes as the Food and Drugs Act 1955, or the Weights and Measures Act 1963 have involved both strict and vicarious liability, and that some offences, under the Licensing Acts for example, have involved vicarious liability even though they were *mens rea* offences. In some few instances statutes have expressly imposed vicarious liability. In most, the court holds that the statute implies such responsibility.[54]

The formulae under which vicarious liability are imposed are not less nebulous that those which apply to strict liability. The accepted formula, which applies both to *mens rea* offences and to those of strict liability, is that of Lord Atkin in *Mousell Brothers Limited* v. *London and North Western Railway Company*. His Lordship stated:[55]

> "While prima facie a principal is not to be made criminally responsible for the acts of his servants, yet the Legislature may prohibit an act or enforce a duty in such words as to make the prohibition or the duty absolute; in which case the principal is in fact liable if the act is in fact done by his servants. To ascertain

whether a particular act of Parliament has that effect or not, regard must be had to the words used, the nature of the duty laid down, the person upon whom it is imposed, the person by whom it would in ordinary circumstances be performed, and the person upon whom the penalty is imposed.''

The decision itself may well be questionable.[56] Lord Atkin's formula does draw attention to the criteria commonly invoked by the courts. In most cases, for example of sale or supplying, the act is done by an employee, a counter clerk or pump attendant or some similar person. The duty may appear to be imposed indifferently upon any person, but courts generally conclude that the intention is to place the duty upon an employer to regulate his enterprise. The employer or the employee may in fact perform the acts to which the duty relates, but the employer is held liable because he as employer can regulate the conduct of employees and himself in the enterprise. Indeed, the nexus might be identified broadly as that of control; sometimes it is satisfied by a course of employment formula, but on other occasions it is satisfied by delegation of managerial functions. This is particularly marked where the offence is one involving *mens rea*, but it is not confined to that instance.[57]

Before considering the question of nexus, it is proposed to deal briefly with the question of *mens rea* offences. We have seen that vicarious liability is imposed in respect of some such offences, either on the basis that the statutory command is addressed specifically to the master or licensee or other designated person so that he alone can commit the offence,[58] or, more broadly, as suggested in *Mousell's* case, because in this as in all instances of vicarious liability the legislation ought to be interpreted as casting the duty on the employer where in all probability the actual physical acts in question will be those of an employee.

The licensee cases ought, even more firmly than when Professor Williams wrote, to be considered anomalous. This was certainly the view of Lord Reid both in *Vane* v. *Yiannopoulos*[59] and in *Tesco Supermarkets Ltd.* v. *Nattrass*.[60] In the former case his Lordship concluded that the existing ambit of vicarious liability ought to be upheld, but certainly not extended. According to Lords Reid and Evershed, the licensee could not be held vicariously liable when, he being on the premises, a *mens rea* offence was committed by his employee without his knowledge; Lords Donovan and Morris took a different view. The Court of Appeal in *Reg.* v. *Winson*[61] concluded that such liability applied only where the statute was specifically addressed to the licensee and he had entirely delegated the management of his premises. Rather surprisingly the Divisional Court in *Howker* v. *Robinson*[62] concluded that vicarious liability for a *mens rea* offence was possible under s.169 of the Licensing Act 1964 which provides that the holder of a licence or his servant shall not knowingly sell intoxicating liquor to a person under eighteen. The effect of the altered wording was said not to exclude vicarious liability, but simply to add the servant as an additional target fit for prosecution. This is, of course, to ignore the entire basis in policy for vicarious responsibility in the licensee cases, though it can, as can almost anything, be brought within Lord Atkin's formulation in *Mousell's* case. In my submission *Howker* v. *Robinson* ought to be regarded as wrongly decided; it is inconsistent with the tenor of their Lordships' speeches in *Vane* v. *Yiannopoulos*, and it cannot be reconciled with *Winson*.

Where strict liability offences are involved, the question whether vicarious liability is intended can be approached in different ways. One such is by what Professor Glanville Williams calls the extensive construction of verbs. The problem, as he states, is one of *actus reus*: it is "to know when the courts will regard a master as doing something, within the meaning of a statute, although the act is actually done by his servant".[63] And the master is regarded as primarily rather than secondarily responsible. In some cases such as the sale of food and drugs, sale can, as he points out, be construed as referring to the physical act of sale or the legal relationship of seller and buyer. The courts throw the net over both the servant who physically sells and the principal who legally sells.

The notion of a judicial dictionary as an explanation is appealing, and its adherents impressive, but, in my submission, it is ultimately unsatisfactory.[64] It is really no more than one device, among others, which courts employ in order to justify the imposition of vicarious liability. It is not really a reason for imposing it, nor does the dual meaning of verbs afford an exclusive test for determining when it is to be imposed. No doubt, where a verb indicates a physical act which is likely to be performed by a servant and which results in a legal relationship between the master and a third party the case for vicarious liability is a strong one, but one cannot really put the matter higher than that. Any catalogue is bound to be arbitrary. The better inquiry would be not into the supposed dual meaning of words, but into whether in context it could sensibly be thought that a duty of supervision was being imposed and whether vicarious liability was neccessary to its enforcement. In many of the vehicle construction and use cases referred to above, the answer would seem to be yes. Inevitably, there will be cases of a difficult character to which no certain answer can be given in advance.

The question of nexus is rather easier to approach. Vicarious liability is not imposed upon a master because the act was done by his servant or in some cases his delegate; the reason for imposing liability is to secure compliance with legislation; the particular *actus reus* is often singled out because it is an objective act which can be proven readily and upon which it is sensible to base liability. Where the actual fault occurred at an earlier stage, an onus is often placed on the accused to show that he ought to be acquitted because he was not truly at fault for the consequence which the law forbids.

The nexus is sometimes course of employment and sometimes delegation. It was thought that these formulations were in competition, and that delegation was the ground which covered all the cases. In fact they seem properly to be overlapping, not conflicting.[65] Delegation is, however, the appropriate test under the licensee cases for obvious reasons; the courts devised liability in such cases in order to ensure that an absentee licensee would not be able to insulate himself from liability in respect of the premises.

So far as the employment relationship is concerned, the liability of the employer extends, it is clear, to acts which he did not authorise and, indeed, forbade.[66]

It is, however, clear that criminal liability is not to be imposed in every instance where an employer would be vicariously liable civilly. *Portsea Island Mutual Cooperative Society Ltd.* v. *Leyland* illustrates the point.[67] Contrary to company instructions, a milk roundsman hired a boy to assist him. The act was done by the roundsman for his employer's business and with intent to benefit the employer, but it was done contrary to the employer's instructions. The company did not employ the boy; it could only be held liable where it employed him either directly or through a properly authorised agent. The fact that a company might, on similar facts, be civilly liable to a lad who suffered injuries while accompanying the roundsman was irrelevant.[68] There is earlier authority to the same effect.[69]

We have said that the formulae of course of employment and delegation overlap. *Barker* v. *Levinson*[70] it has been suggested, illustrates a conflict between them and, it has confidently been argued, delegation covers the whole ground.[71] It is true that in the authorised report of that case, the Lord Chief Justice explained vicarious liability as resting upon the nexus of delegation. Two points can be made about this. The first is that delegation is not an apt expression to describe the sort of authority normally enjoyed by an employee, and even an agent, other perhaps than a managing agent. Delegation, it has been said, does not mean the same thing as employment. Thus Wrottesley L.J., in a civil action stated:[72]

> "An employer does not, merely by employing his servant to work a crane, delegate to him the statutory duty of seeing that the crane is not overloaded."

Delegation, surely, involves a bestowal of managerial functions. It is thus the right word to describe the licensee cases, but hardly the ordinary sale cases. Secondly, the courts in the general run of cases have continued to use the notion of course of employment to describe the requisite nexus.[73] Furthermore, there is no reason to suppose that delegation and course of employment are the only nexuses available. A partner may be be held liable for the acts of his fellow partner.[74] A licensee will be liable for an unlawful act of sale by his staff even though they are not his employees but those of the owner, since the licensee is alone reponsible for ensuring adherence to licensing legislation.[75] If a shop owner were to ask his son to serve customers while he attended to stock, there seems no reason to refrain from imputing an act of sale to the owner notwithstanding that there was no contractual relationship between him and his son. The ultimate question ought to be whether the proprietor has control over the actions of the other, and there seems no reason to insist that such control be contractual in character.

The courts have interpreted the legislation in this sense, and they have not allowed themselves to be seduced by a nexus argument which would defeat enforcement of the legislation. Nor have they excused an employer whose servant intended to benefit himself. It has been suggested that there ought not to be liability where the servant, in committing the infraction, acted in his own interests and not in the purported interests of the master.[76] It is submitted that this is wrong. Vicarious liability exists in order to ensure that employers and others to whom it applies will police their businesss. The question whom the offender intended to benefit is irrelevant viewed from that perspective. This is even clearer when the positive defences, discussed in chapter 4 are considered; whether a defence is available or not, depends upon, and only upon, whether the particular steps outlined in the legislation are followed. The question of intent to benefit does not appear in the schemes.

NOTES

[1] *E.g. Hobbs* v. *Winchester Corporation* [1910] 2 K.B, 471; *Reg.* v. *St. Margaret's Trust Ltd.* [1958] 1 W.L.R. 522

[2] *Reg.* v. *Howells* [1977] Q.B. 614.

[3] *Reg.* v. *Miller* [1977] 1 W.L.R. 1129.

[4] *Albert* v. *Lavin* [1981] 1 All E.R. 628.

[5] [1895] 1 Q.B. 918.

[6] J. Hall, *General Principles of Criminal Law* (2 ed. 1960), pp. 330–331.

[7] Companies Act, 1980, ss.68–73 and L.H. Leigh, *The Control of Commercial Fraud* (1982), pp. 112–120 for a summary.

[8] *Sherras* v. *de Rutzen, supra.*

[9] [1970] A.C. 132.

[10] Whether such acts are or are not to be considered as crimes is a vexed question. I prefer, following Lord Atkin in *Proprietary Articles Trade Association* v. *A.G. Canada* [1931] A.C. 310 to view that conduct as criminal which Parliament punishes through the medium of the criminal law. See further, G. L. Williams, "The Definition of Crime" (1955) *C.L.P.* 107.

[11] [1970] A.C. 132 at p. 156.

[12] *Ibid.* p. 163.

[13] [1969] 2 A.C. 256 at p. 271.

[14] [1972] A.C. 153 at p. 194.

[15] [1978] 2 S.C.R. 1299 at pp. 1302–3.

[16] *Lim Chin Aik* v. *Reginam* [1963] A.C. 161; *Sweet* v. *Parsley* [1970] A.C. 132 at p. 163 *per* Lord Diplock, and the judgment of Devlin J. (as he then was) in *Reynolds* v. *G.H. Austin & Sons Ltd.* [1951] 2 K.B. 135 at p. 150.

[17] As was the case in *Lim Chin Aik* v. *Reginam, supra.* *Reg.* v. *Larsonneur* (1933) 97 J.P. 206, is an obvious exception to this, but its status as an authority must as we have argued surely now be doubtful.

[18] n. 16, *supra.*

[19] Chapter 6, *post.*

[20] This was early recognised by Lord Devlin, *Samples of Lawmaking*, (1952).

[21] (1885) 16 Q.B.D. 190; see also *Rex* v. *Hudson* [1943] 1 K.B. 458.

[22] [1938] 1 K.B. 505.

[23] [1969] 2 A.C. 256; for amending legislation see Misuse of Drugs Act 1971, esp. s.28 which creates affirmative defences.

[24] This refers to the proviso to s.2(1) of the Criminal Appeal Act 1968, by which an appeal may be dismissed, even though there was an error in the court below, on the ground that in fact no miscarriage of justice actually occurred.

[25] [1969] 2 A.C. 256 at p.306 *per* Lord Pearce.

[26] [1981] Crim.L.R. 251.

[27] [1971] S.C.R. 5.

[28] *Beaver* v. *The Queen* [1957] S.C.R. 531.

[29] For an early and comprehensive account, see J. Ll. J. Edwards, *Mens Rea in Statutory Offences* (1955).

[30] *Sweet* v. *Parsley* [1970] A.C. 132 at p. 162; *Reg.* v. *Souter* [1972] 2 All E.R. 1151.

[31] *Reg.* v. *Thomas* (1976) 63 Cr.App.R. 65.

[32] *Criminal Law, the General Part* (2 ed. 1961), p. 164.

[33] *Grays Haulage Co. Ltd.* v. *Arnold* [1966] 1 W.L.R. 534; *P. Lowery & Sons Ltd.* v. *Wark* [1975] R.T.R. 45 D.C.; *Evans* v. *Dell* [1937] 1 All E.R. 349; the term includes wilful blindness, see *Smith of Middleton Ltd.* v. *MacNab*, 1975, S.L.T. (J). 85.

[34] *Baugh* v. *Crago* [1975] R.T.R. 453; *Tapsell* v. *Maslin* [1967] Crim.L.R. 53 D.C.; *Lyons* v. *May* [1948] 2 All E.R. 1062.

[35] *Ferrymasters Ltd.* v. *Adams* [1980] R.T.R. 139.

[36] *Baugh* v. *Crago, supra*; *Newbury* v. *Davis* [1974] R.T.R. 367.

[37] See discussion by Herring C.J. in *Broadhurst* v. *Paul* [1954] V.L.R. 541.

[38] [1972] A.C. 824.

[39] *Wurzel* v. *Wilson* [1965] 1 W.L.R. 285.

[40] *Lovelace* v. *D.P.P.* [1954] 3 All E.R. 481; the offence in question has been superseded by the Theatres Act 1968.

[41] *Cox and Sons Ltd.* v. *Sidery* (1935) 24 R. & T.C. 69.

[42] *Ross-Hillman Ltd.* v. *Bond* [1974] 1 Q.B. 435; *Houston* v. *Buchanan* 1940 S.L.T. 232 (H.L.); *cf. Smith of Middleton Ltd.* v. *McNab*, 1975, S.L.T. (J) 8.

[43] *Sopp* v. *Long* [1970] 1 Q.B. 518

[44] *James and Son Ltd.* v. *Smee* [1955] 1 Q.B. 78.

[45] *Windle* v. *Dunning and Son Ltd.* [1968] 2 All E.R. 46; *Carmichael & Sons (Worcester) Ltd.* v. *Cottle* (1970) 114 S.J. 866.

[46] *Pioneer Express Pty. Ltd.* v. *Hotchkiss* (1958) 101 C.L.R. 536; *Jackson* v. *Horne* (1965) 114 C.L.R. 82; *Winston Transport Pty. Ltd.* v. *Horne* (1965) 115 C.L.R. 322; and see *Windle* v. *Dunning & Son Ltd.* [1968] Crim.L.R. 337.

[47] [1948] 1 K.B. 695.

[48] *Chajutin* v. *Whitehead* [1938] 1 K.B. 506.

[49] per Lord Reid in *Warner* v. *Metropolitan Police Commissioner* [1969] 2 A.C. 256 at p. 278.

[50] (1974) 16 K.I.R. 220.

[51] [1975] 2 All E.R. 974.

[52] See *Allan* v. *Patterson* [1980] R.T.R. 97.

[53] It has been suggested that vicarious liability does not exist; see P. Glazebrook, "Situational Liability", in Glazebrook (ed.), *Reshaping the Criminal Law* (1978); the argument about whether liability should be called vicarious seems to me to be largely semantic.

[54] G. L. Williams, *Criminal Law, The General Part* (2 ed. 1961), p. 269.

[55] [1917] 2 K.B. 836.

[56] G. L. Williams, *op. cit.* p. 274.

[57] See further, D. Rose, "Vicarious Liability in Statutory Offences", (1971) 45 *A.L.J.* 252; L.H. Leigh, "Statutory Offences and Vicarious Criminal Liability" (1964) 27 M.L.R. 98.

[58] In addition to cases cited *ante* see the Scottish cases of *Glasgow Corporation* v. *Strathern*, 1929, J.C. 5; *Graham* v. *Strathern*, 1927 J.C. 29.

[59] [1965] A.C. 486.

[60] [1972] A.C. 153 at p. 169.

[61] [1968] 1 All E.R. 197, C.A.

[62] [1972] 2 All E.R. 786.

[63] G. L. Williams, *op. cit.*, pp. 273–284.

[64] G. L. Williams, *op. cit.*, at p. 281; P. Glazebrook, *loc. cit.* also supports this explanation.

[65] D. Rose, *loc. cit.*

[66] *e.g. C.P.R.* v. *Lockhart* [1942] A.C. 591 (P.C.); *Ward* v. *W. H. Smith & Sons Ltd.* [1913] 3 K.B. 154; *Griffith* v. *Studebakers Ltd.* [1924] 1 K.B. 102; *Anderton* v. *Rogers* [1981] Crim.L.R. 404; *Rex* v. *Piggly Wiggly Canadian Limited* [1933] 4 D.L.R. 491; *cf. Anglo-American Oil Company* v. *Manning* [1908] 1 K.B. 536.

[67] [1978] I.C.R. 1195.

[68] *Rose* v. *Plenty* [1975] I.C.R. 430.

[69] *Star Cinema (Shepherds Bush) Ltd.* v. *Baker* (1921) 86 J.P. 47.

[70] [1951] 1 K.B. 342; [1950] 2 All E.R. 825; see also *Quality Dairies (York) Ltd.* v. *Pedley* [1952] 1 K.B. 275.

[71] J. Ll. L. Edwards, *op. cit.*, chapter 10.

[72] *Gallagher* v. *Dorman Long and Co. Ltd.* [1947] 2 All E.R. 35 at p. 41.

[73] *e.g. Winter* v. *Hinckley* [1959] 1 W.L.R. 182; *Tesco Supermarkets Ltd.* v. *Nattrass* [1972] A.C. 153; *Reg.* v. *Winson* [1969] 1 Q.B. 371; *Anderton* v. *Rogers* [1981] Crim.L.R. 404, and further, see D. Rose, *loc. cit.*

[74] *Clode* v. *Barnes* [1974] 1 All E.R. 1166.
[75] *Goodfellow* v. *Johnson* [1966] 1 Q.B. 83.
[76] *Navarro* v. *Moregrand* [1951] 2 T.L.R. 674 at p. 681 *per* Denning L.J.; the suggestion is clearly inconsistent with *Rex* v. *I.C.R. Haulage Ltd.* [1944] K.B. 551 which, although on corporate liability, is permeated with vicarious liability concepts.

Chapter 4

THE FAULT PRINCIPLE AND DEFENCES

We have seen that liability is normally strict, rather than absolute. English law and practice does, in fact, take account of fault in the enforcement of the law. It does so in three ways; through common law defences, through statutory defences, and through discretion to prosecute. In the latter two instances, in particular, it does so with regard to the purposes of statutory schemes. It is not surprising that fault should find a prominent place in the administration of the law. It is no doubt necessary that in some cases the prosecution should not have to prove a culpable state of mind in order to procure a conviction. Nonetheless, the law can, sensibly, take account of an absence of fault either generally, as through a common law due diligence defence, or more particularly through statutory defences which direct one's attention to the steps which it is desired the defendant should take in order to avoid contravention and conviction. This latter mode of legislating is not, as we have seen, confined to petty offences, for obvious practical reasons.[1] Again, discretion to prosecute may be and often is exercised on a view of fault, even though statutory defences, which also express the fault principle, apply to the case.

Common Law Defences

English law has never developed a general due diligence defence. In this, it contrasts markedly with Australian and Canadian law. There are particular instances of no fault defences in the law, but they remain as isolated fragments.

It is perhaps surprising that common law "no fault" defences succeed most often in motor vehicle cases. It is in just this area that strict liability is least often mitigated by statutory defences, but at the same time, the evident dangers which the careless operation of vehicles present tend to render the courts cautious in affording scope for excuses. In the result, defences have been recognised, but they are narrowly expressed and fragmented. Furthermore, the relationship between strict liability and general common law defences such as duress, necessity and even mistake, has not been worked out with any particularity.

The offence of dangerous driving has been abolished and replaced by that of reckless driving.[2] The cases which established that the former offence was not an absolute offence remain, nonetheless, of importance to strict liability generally. It is clear, for example, that the defence is not restricted to automatism, in the sense of a sudden loss of control which deprives the act of driving of its voluntary character. In the latest case to pronounce upon these matters, *Roberts* v. *Ramsbottom*[3] which involved a civil claim for damages, Neill J., speaking of the criminal cases, held that dangerous driving was not an absolute offence, but rather one to which fault applied. Fault indicates a falling below the care and skill of a competent and experienced driver in relation to the driving and other relevant circumstances of the case. A sudden event may provide a defence, for example, a sudden mechanical defect, or an epileptic fit, or coma, or being struck by a stone or assailed by a swarm of bees. In some of these cases, the accused may be regarded as not driving at all. Where, however, the accused retains some power of control and some consciousness, albeit clouded, he is to be regarded as driving, and dangerously at that.

It is difficult to assimilate all the cases to a common basis, as *Roberts* v. *Ramsbottom* indeed indicates. The no fault principle clearly goes beyond cases where there was no willed act, into a variety of other cases where the accused was not at fault and, indeed, could not readily have done more to ensure compliance with the law. In *Reg.* v. *Gosney*[4] the court held admissible defence evidence, on a charge of dangerous driving, which tended to show that there was no indication at an intersection which would have warned a careful driver like the accused, that she was about to turn into the wrong lane of a dual carriageway. It disapproved a statement in the unsatisfactory case of *Reg.* v. *Ball and Loughlin*[5] to the effect that a good driver who did his best in difficult circumstances could nonetheless be convicted of the offence. In *Reg.* v. *Spurge*[6] it was held that a sudden mechanical defect might serve as a defence. It could not truly be said that the driving created the danger; it was the occasion, but not the cause. The court, however, noted that the defect must be one which was not known to the driver and which could not have been discovered by him with reasonable care. This principle was rapidly qualified by the courts. In *Leicester* v. *Pearson*,[7] it had been held that a driver who failed to accord precedence to a foot passenger could be acquitted where the magistrates found that the driver was exercising all due care, keeping a proper look-out, and was driving without negligence. The accident occurred because the driver, through no fault of his own, failed to see the pedestrian. Such cases, where the magistrates can find an entire absence of fault, are rare. In *Burns* v. *Bidder*[8] the case was explained on this ground; the driver was acquitted because his control of the vehicle was taken from him by the occurrence of an event which was outside his possible and reasonable control. In the New Zealand decision of *Police* v. *Creedon*,[9] Richmond J. concluded that the cases could be reconciled on the basis that a defence is open only to a prudent and careful driver who can show that it was impossible for him to have done more to comply with the regulation. Furthermore, where sudden defect is alleged, it must be latent, and undiscoverable by reasonable care. A later court held, in a case in which the justices were clear that the driver must have known of the defect because he had complained of it when taking the car in for servicing, that the most a prudent driver can assume under such circumstances is that a service was carried out; he cannot, without more, assume that the defect was rectified, and he could not, therefore, rely on a defect attributable to it as sudden and unforeseen.[10] The case does not say what the result would be where the driver was explicitly assured that the defect had been discovered and rectified; the facts here did not go so far.

Finally, in this vein, we may note the ambiguous case of *Friend* v. *Western British Road Services Ltd.*[11] That case involved Reg. 92 of the Motor Vehicles (Construction and Use) Regulations 1973, which provided that a vehicle load must be so secured as to ensure that no danger shall be caused to any person by reason of the load falling from the vehicle. A load of steel coils fell from the defendant's vehicle causing danger. The evidence disclosed that the defendant had used the safest known means of loading, that a little understood phenomenon known as "slow roll-over" was involved, and that any other method of loading would have caused the vehicle to roll over as well. The court acquitted the defendant, but its reasoning is obscure. Clearly, it accepted that there was an absence of fault on the part of the defendant. The case may be explained either as turning on an absence of fault or, as the editor of the Criminal Law Review suggests, as turning on the proposition that roll over is so rare that danger was not likely to be caused by the manner of loading the cargo, or the particular method used in the case. Whether, however, the case turns on general principle or on the construction of particular words, the offence is not absolute. Furthermore, either route may be open to the defence in any given case.

Absence of fault is, however, not a fully articulated defence in English law. This has already been noted in chapter 1, in considering the definition of strict liability, and in relation to offences involving possession of drugs. It also applies to the possession of firearms where an honest and reasonable belief that an article was an antique, rather than a (reproduction) firearm, was held not to be a defence to a charge of possession of a firearm without a certificate.[12] And of course there are instances under road traffic legislation itself where absence of fault does not avail the accused. *Reg.* v. *Bowsher*[13] is a harsh example of this; the accused who had been disqualified by two successive courts and who was not told that the disqualifications were consecutive, applied for and received his licence back prematurely. He was duly convicted of driving while disqualified, even though he was not at fault. This case evidences that there is no general "no fault" defence under Road Traffic legislation: it would be implausible to regard it as an exception to such a general defence. On the other hand, Lord Diplock in *Sweet* v. *Parsley* suggested that a general due diligence defence might be possible at common law.[14] We have noted the existence of such a defence in Australia and Canada. It is appropriate at this juncture to examine its antecedents and extent, before considering the question upon what basis it might be introduced into English law.

The Australian formulation derives from *Proudman* v. *Dayman*.[15] The charge was that the accused permitted a person, not being the holder of a licence for the time being in force, to drive a motor vehicle on a public road. The question arose whether the accused could raise a defence of honest and reasonable mistake to the charge. Although on the facts there was no basis for such a defence, Dixon, J. held that reasonable mistake might be raised as a defence to a charge of a strict liability offence. The reasoning adopted by His Honour was that a holding that the prosecution need not prove intention or recklessness to procure a conviction does not imply that fault has no part in the case. His Honour thus states:[16]

> "It is one thing to deny that a necessary ingredient of the offence is positive knowledge of the fact that the driver holds no subsisting licence. It is another to say that an honest belief founded on reasonable grounds that he is licensed cannot exculpate a person who

permits him to drive. As a general rule an honest and reasonable belief in a state of facts which, if they existed, would make the defendant's act innocent affords an excuse for doing what would otherwise be an offence."

From this it followed that, save in an exceptional case where liability is truly intended to be absolute, the accused might defend himself by showing that he exercised due diligence to comply with the law. The affinity of this thought to those English cases which insisted that an absence of *mens rea* words simply shifted the burden of proof is plain.

The result of this approach is to create three categories of statutory offences; those in which the prosecution must prove full *mens rea*; those in which it need not prove *mens rea* but the accused may raise as a defence to a charge that he or she exercised all due diligence; and those in which liability is absolute. In this latter case, the legislature must make it clear that absolute liability is intended.[17]

It is impossible to indicate what view English courts will ultimately take of the place of fault as a common law principle. In *Sweet* v. *Parsley* Lords Reid, Pearce and Diplock intimated that the question of due diligence defences may not be entirely foreclosed by authority. In *Reg.* v. *Warner*, Lord Guest had thought that the half-way house represented by the Australian cases was blocked by the decision in *Woolmington* v. *D.P.P.*,[18] that the Crown must prove, beyond a reasonable doubt, all the elements of the case. In *Sweet* v. *Parsley*, Lord Diplock intimates that this point may need to be reconsidered; *Woolmington*, his Lordship states, is no bar to the use of honest and reasonable mistake as a solvent of strict liability cases since it only decides that where there is evidence of a defence, a jury must consider it and acquit the accused unless they are sure that the accused did not hold a particular belief, or there were no reasonable grounds for it.

Dicta in *Morgan* also suggest that a common law no

fault defence is possible, but they are very confused.[19] The *ratio* of the case is that in rape, an honest mistake as to the existence of the elements of the offence is a defence. The House of Lords was, however, obliged to explain away a series of cases on bigamy which held that a mistake had both to be honest and reasonable to afford a defence. Lord Cross drew a distinction between offences which require *mens rea* and those which do not. Some *mens rea* offences specify the mental element required for the offence; in respect of them, mistake need only be honest. Other *mens rea* offences do not specify any mental element; in their case, mistake must be both honest and reasonable.[20] Where no *mens rea* is required at all, mistake will not excuse the defendant. On this view, a mistake defence would only be available where a court was prepared to construe an offence which is silent as to the mental element, as involving *mens rea*. Why there should be a difference between two classes of *mens rea* offences is obscure. Lord Hailsham took a different view of the bigamy cases. He treated the leading case, *Tolson*,[21] as a narrow decision based on the construction of a statute which *prima facie* appeared to create an absolute offence subject to a statutory defence related to a seven year period of absence. His Lordship suggests this explanation:[22]

> "The judges . . . decided that this was not reasonable, and, on general jurisprudential principles, imported into the statutory offence words which created a special 'defence' of honest and reasonable belief of which the 'evidential', but not the probative burden lay on the defence."

If Lord Hailsham's suggestion were adopted, there would be no reason why honest and reasonable mistake, or a showing by the accused that he used due diligence to comply with the law, should not afford a defence to crimes of strict liability generally, subject always to the power of

Parliament to legislate so as to exclude it. If the general jurisprudential principle referred to (whatever it may be) can be invoked to prevent injustice in one case, there seems no reason why it could not be invoked in another. No doubt a tendency to do so would be most marked where a penalty of imprisonment was available and sometimes imposed for the offence, or where the stigma attaching to conviction for that offence was very considerable. Where the usual penalty was a fine, an inference that no such defence was intended might well be drawn, as it might where an adequate statutory scheme of defences was already provided. But all these are possibilities latent in *dicta* in leading cases; no court has sought to build upon them. It cannot be said with certainty, therefore, whether the courts will continue to recognise defences based upon particular statutory words, or whether they will take the further step of creating a general due diligence defence which would be displaced only where a particular scheme made it clear that no such defence was intended. There is, of course, the further point that the common law development may be overtaken by statute, should the Law Commission's proposals be enacted.

It is worth sketching the outlines of the Canadian and Australian position, simply in order to indicate what the implications would be for England and Wales if the courts were to adopt a general due diligence defence. We have noted that the result is to create three categories of offence. Clearly, few provisions would be found to require absolute liability. Canadian and Australian courts consider that absolute liability is unlikely to produce a higher standard of care than would liability based on an absence of due diligence. It is therefore, unlikely that many schemes would be found to require it. The likely result of importing Australian doctrine is that such words as "permitting" and "causing" would more readily be found to import strict liability subject to a due diligence defence, in effect placing an evidentiary burden on the defence over a wider range of matters than at present. Furthermore, the due diligence defence would most probably apply to such matters as road traffic where an elaborate scheme of statutory defences does not apply. In many other cases, the defences would continue to apply in their present terms and there would not seem to be room for a special due diligence defence.

Other possible refinements may be indicated. In Australia, some courts recognise not only a no negligence defence, but also that the harm was caused by the act of a stranger. The leading case appears to be *Boucher* v. *G. J. Coles & Co. Ltd.*[23] The accused was charged with having kept for sale a can of peas which was intended for human consumption and was unsound, contrary to s.111(1) of the Health Act, 1935–72. The unsoundness was the fault of the supplier. The magistrate found that the accused could not be liable because the product ordered from the supplier, sound peas, was not the product which was supplied. The court reversed the decision. It treats the section as imposing strict liability. The "act of a stranger" defence applies generally, whether a crime is a crime of strict liability or not. It is justified by the premise that there is nothing the accused can do to take further care in the circumstances; the legislature does not demand the impossible. It could not apply in this case because the event was not an uncontemplated event in the sense of an action by a person whose intrusion or the manner of whose intrusion into the situation was something not reasonably to be expected or foreseen. Careless packing is not an incalculable event. So far as this aspect of the case is concerned, the defence of "act of a stranger" appears to be a particular application of the rule that criminal responsibility requires a voluntary act or omission by the accused. It appears to go farther than conventional expressions of that rule, because it can render blameless an act done by the accused, where the circumstance rendering it unlawful was not attributable to his fault. Thus the *actus reus* here was keeping unsound peas for sale; the relevance of the defence was not to negate the action of keeping, but rather to negate any element of blame for the fact of unsoundness. So viewed, it could, where the accused really is fault free, apply to many cases where the *actus reus* is specified to lie in sale or possession of an article in an unsatisfactory state, to negate guilt. It does not appear to have been developed in English law where, over a wide range of strict liability offences, there are statutory provisions applying affirmative defences based, in part, upon the fault being that of a person other than the accused.

There is a further point on the due diligence defence itself. While the defence is expressed in general terms, the court can tailor it, in particular cases, to the exigencies of the activity regulated, and can, for example, insist on proper inspection standards for regulated industries. Once again, over a wide range of strict liability offences, United Kingdom legislation makes provision for such matters. The need for judicial initiatives is accordingly reduced.

Statutory Defences

We turn, therefore, to consider statutory defences. These are widespread in the area of public welfare offences, but they are by no means universally provided, and their absence in particular legislation is not necessarily attributable either to legislative forgetfulness or impercipience. Some statutes do not have wide due diligence defences, and their insertion is sometimes strongly resisted. Fisheries legislation appears to attract narrowly expressed defences, for example. Under both the Sea Fish (England and Wales) Act, 1980, and legislation relating to the importation of live fish, the defence to various offences connected with over-fishing is a narrowly expressed exemption for operations of a scientific nature.[24] It seems clear enough in the former case that masters or owners of fishing vessels are not to be allowed to shuffle off responsibility onto others, nor may importers do so in the latter case. Similarly, no defence is provided for unauthorised dumping, contrary to the Refuse Disposal (Amenity) Act 1978. Underlying statutes of this character is the notion that defences, cast in terms of due diligence, may make it too easy for the accused to avoid liability, thus frustrating the purposes of the Act. There are, it must be said, areas where control has been difficult, and where it would be singularly difficult to disprove due diligence. For this reason, the government was unwilling to insert such defences in the lapsed Protection of the Environment Bill 1974, despite persuasion by the Law Commission to do so.[25] The government thought the matter best left to prosecutors' discretion.[26]

There is a point worth emphasising here. The justification for absolute liability, rather than strict liability subject to a due diligence defence, cannot, surely, be that absolute liability conduces to greater care in a way that strict liability does not. The problem rather is that in some areas the burden of proving that an accused did not exercise due diligence, would be well-nigh impossible for the prosecution to discharge. Enforcement would, if such a defence were provided, become too difficult, and great harm would result from contravention. Hence the individual is virtually made an insurer of his conduct, subject perhaps to very narrowly expressed defences of the sort outlined above. Problems of pollution have certainly been viewed in these terms.[27] Legislation dealing with poisons is stricter still. An employer whose employee sells or supplies poisons in contravention of the Poisons Rules cannot defend himself by showing that the employee acted contrary to orders, and any material fact known to the employee is deemed to be known to the employer.[28] Again, the employer is made an insurer of his enterprise.

Defences of Necessity

Legislative provision is sometimes made for cases of necessity even where defences are otherwise narrowly expressed or not provided. For example, the Dumping at

Sea Act 1974 gives a defence to an accused who proves that substances were dumped for the purpose of securing the safety of a ship. This is, however, made subject to an obligation to notify the minister of what was done. The accused may, furthermore, still be convicted if the court is satisfied that the dumping was not done for the purposes specified in the statute, and was not a reasonable step to take under the circumstances.[29] Similarly, under the Slaughterhouses Act 1974, it is a defence to an alleged contravention of the legislation for an accused to prove that because of an accident or other emergency, the contravention was necessary for preventing physical injury or suffering to any person or animal.[30]

Defences of necessity are also provided to some road traffic offences. For example, it is a defence to a driver of a vehicle used for fire brigade, police or ambulance purposes who exceeds the speed limit, that the observance of that limit would be likely to hinder the use of the vehicle for the purpose for which it was being used on that occasion.[31] Under regulations concerning road crossings, it is a defence for a driver to stop within the limits of the crossing where he is prevented from proceeding either by circumstances beyond his control, or in order to avoid an accident.[32]

Statutory defences of this sort are strictly construed against the motorist. In *Oakley-Moore* v. *Robinson*[33] the Divisional Court held that a motorist who had run out of petrol could not rely on the statutory defence when he parked his car within the prohibited approach limits to a pelican crossing. There were two bases to the decision. The first is that there was a reserve petrol tank in the car of which the accused failed to inform himself. The second, far broader, is that although the defence would have been available had the driver been prevented from proceeding by a sudden mechanical defect, a lack of petrol did not fall within that category. Though stringent, the decision can readily be supported on the basis that it is the duty of the driver to ensure that he does not run out of petrol and that

duty is not difficult to discharge, save in wholly exceptional circumstances. Another stringent, but correct decision,
is *Higgins* v. *Bernard*.[34] The accused, who stopped on a
motorway shoulder because he was too tired to continue
was held not to be entitled to rely on a defence based on
the existence of an emergency. He knew before he
entered the motorway that he was fatigued. The defence
only applies, the court held, where the emergency arises
after the person has commenced driving on the motorway.
It need not be a sudden emergency, however; it is enough
that some event occurs which makes it dangerous for the
driver to proceed. But this, though correct, is harsh, and it
might well produce the bad result that drivers, fearing
conviction, will continue to drive when they should not.

Due diligence defences usually stress two aspects of the
defendant's conduct, namely, whether the infraction was
due to the act or default of another person, and whether
the defendant exercised due diligence to prevent the
infraction. There is, however, considerable variation in
the wording employed, and the reason for this is that the
statutory schemes in question themselves vary consider-
ably. While such defences have, as noted, been in force
since the late nineteenth century, we take account here
only of modern examples.

The precise structure of statutory defences depends
upon the scheme to which they relate. In general,
however, they include the two components noted above.
In legislation there is a tendency to fasten on such acts as
sale as representing the choice of an *actus reus* of
convenience.[35] It is at this point that the legislation
primarily bites, and for obvious reasons. It is the first
external manifestation of fault. Of course fault can occur
from the inception of the manufacturing process to the
point of sale, but it is at the latter stage that it becomes
manifest. If the case is one of retail sale, the retailer, if not
truly at fault himself, can at least indicate who the persons
in the chain are, and by showing his own blamelessness,
help to indicate who the real culprit is. There is also an

obvious tendency to protect mere employees whose default is due to their employer's instructions. In such case the employee may be able to avoid conviction by showing that he acted in compliance with such instructions.[36]

Statutory schemes, therefore, reflect these themes, but they vary in their details. Some enable defendants to rely on warranties from their supplier. Others enable the defendant to rely on the acts of a third party who is primarily responsible for ensuring the integrity of a scheme.[37] Some place high, some less onerous obligations upon the defendant to shift fault. Some enable the prosecution to proceed directly against a person or body who is deemed to be the principal offender. Virtually all indicate with some particularity what steps the accused must take in order to demonstrate his want of fault, and in this respect they set out a more precise set of procedures than might be required by a general due diligence defence.

The leading modern examples of such defences are contained in the Weights and Measures Act 1963, the Food and Drugs Act 1955, and the Trade Descriptions Act 1968. The former Act, for example, gives an employee a defence to a charge of using false weighing or measuring equipment that he used it in the course of his employment with some other person, and that he neither knew, nor might reasonably have been expected to know, nor had any reason to suspect, the equipment to be false or unjust.[38] The effect of this provision is to exculpate the innocent employee, but not one who was in effect the accomplice of his employer. The onus of proof lies upon the employee. With respect to the sale of pre-packaged goods where the fault is most likely to be that of the manufacturer or an intermediate supplier, a three-fold structure of defences applies. It is a defence for the person charged to prove that he bought the goods from some other person as being of the quantity which the person charged purported to sell or represented, or which was marked on any container or stated in any document to which the proceedings relate or as conforming to any regulation applicable to such sale. The accused must further show that he bought the goods with a written warranty from his supplier that they were of the appropriate quantity or did conform to the requirements concerning such goods. Where proceedings concern the quantity of such goods, he must show that he took all reasonable steps to ensure that while the goods were in his possession their quantity remained unchanged, and that apart from any change in quantity, the goods were in the same state at the time of the offence as when he bought them.[39]

The defence of acting under warranty could impede the efficient enforcement of the scheme. It is, therefore, hedged about by restrictive conditions. In the first place, the defendant must notify the prosecution in advance that he proposes to rely upon a warranty and of the name and address of the person emitting it, and he must notify the issuer accordingly, who may attend the hearing and give evidence.[40] A person who gives a false warranty commits an offence unless he proves that when he gave the warranty he took all reasonable steps to ensure that the statements contained in it were and would continue at all relevant times to be accurate.[41] It is clear from this that the giving of a false warranty is simply the giving of a warranty that is false; there is no need to prove that the person giving it knew it to be false. But it is a defence affirmatively to prove due care in the terms required by the statute.

The catalogue of defences by no means ends there. A person may also prove that the commission of the offence was due to a mistake or to an accident or to some other cause beyond his control, a phrase which, it is clear, cannot refer to his employee, for he must show in addition that he took all reasonable precautions and exercised all due diligence to avoid the commission of such an offence in respect of those goods by himself or any person under his control.[42] Defences are also provided in respect of the shrinkage of made up goods.[43] But, and again the legislature addresses the theme of foreseeability, it is not a defence to prove that commission of the offence was due to some factor beyond the defendant's control, if that cause was one which could reasonably have been fore-seen, and for which allowance could reasonably have been made in stating the quantity of the goods or in making up or making the goods.[44]

The Weights and Measures Act 1963 also contains characteristic provisions concerning offences which are due to the default of a third person. The person charged may, upon giving the requisite notice to the prosecution, have the person to whose act or default he alleges the contravention was attributable brought before the court. Then, once commission of the offence is proven, the defendant may exculpate himself by proving that it was due to the act or default of that other person.[45]

This part of the machinery is cumbersome and, in my submission, unjust. It requires the defendant to prove the guilt of the third party beyond a reasonable doubt, for it says that if the defendant proves the guilt of the third party, the latter may be convicted of the offence.[46] Under the very similar machinery of s.113 of the Food and Drugs Act 1955, the accused must prove both limbs of the defence. This involves that he act as prosecutor of the person who he contends is actually at fault; he must prove his case against the actual offender before he can be exculpated.[47] Indeed, under that Act if all the accused can show is that the offending goods were supplied to him by another, both are regarded as guilty of the offence.[48] Thus, not only must the accused prove the guilt of another, but he must further prove that he exercised all due diligence to avoid the commission of the offence by himself or any person under his control. This is, of course, a heavy onus to place upon the accused, and it may also be unworkable from a trade point of view, for it virtually requires a retailer to convict his supplier.[49] It is thus satisfactory that the prosecuting authority can short-circuit these procedures by taking action directly against the offender.[50] Such procedure also applies for example, under s.24 of the Fair Trading Act 1973 and under s.25 of the Slaughterhouse Act 1974. But not the least puzzling aspect of this part of the legislation is that the provision which applies to Scotland is much simpler, for it but requires the offender to establish due diligence and that the offence was attributable to the fault of another.[51] There are further like defences in respect of goods emanating from abroad, but it does not seem necessary to dwell upon their details here.[52] Under the Weights and Measures Act 1979 concerning packaged goods, there are further due diligence defences.

In turn the pattern contained in such legislation as that above was adopted in another prominent consumer protection measure, the Trades Description Acts 1968–1972.[53] Thus s.24 of the 1968 Act provides that an accused may defend himself by proving that the commission of an offence was due to a mistake, an accident or some other cause beyond his control, and that he exercised due diligence to avoid commission of the offence. He also has a third party defence, roughly in the terms noted above in respect of Weights and Measures legislation. We shall have occasion to look at some of the case law under these provisions.

There are many other examples of such provisions, and, it is clear that they are progressively being refined. Examples can be found in the Fair Trading Act 1973 which in addition to due diligence and third party defences, contains defences of innocent publication for a person in the business of publishing advertisements,[54] and in the Consumer Credit Act 1974 where, however, it does not seem to be necessary for the defendant to prove to the criminal standard that the crime was attributable to the third person.[55] The Transport Act 1980 affords a rationalisation of such defences. In respect of one group of offences, it is a defence for an accused to prove that there was a reasonable excuse for the act or omission with which he was charged. In respect of others, an affirmative

showing of all due diligence is required.[56] Assignment of
an offence to one category or the other does appear to
reflect the application of a system. Thus the due diligence
defences apply to infractions which could he committed by
the licensee, or by his employee without his knowledge.
The question whether a system of controls to prevent
infractions both worked and was enforced would thus be
important. Offences falling within this category include
breach or contraventions of conditions relating to a road
service licence, for example concerning routes, fares and
the like, using vehicles in respect of which no certificate of
fitness has been issued, using a vehicle for certain classes
of carriage otherwise than under the authority of a public
service vehicle operator's licence, failing to keep accounts
and records, and the like. "Reasonable excuse", which
seems to refer to cases where the failure must be that of
the accused alone includes certain failures to provide
particulars and information, and may, in certain respects
comprehend what amounts to a defence of necessity. At
present, one would not wish to attribute an absolute
principle of demarcation between the two groups of
offences, but there is, it is submitted, a rough principle in
the sense outlined above.

It is noteworthy that, where road traffic legislation is in
issue, neither set of defences applies to offences concerning the mechanical safety of vehicles or the manner in
which they are driven. It is of course true that occasionally
the courts permit defences in respect of sudden emergen-
cies and the like, but, as we have noted, no general
principle has as yet emerged.

We must now consider how these statutory defences
have been dealt with by the courts. We commence with
the way in which courts have construed the due diligence
defence. The cases make it plain that the courts have for
the most part required a defendant who seeks to make out
an affirmative defence to show that he exercised a high
degree of care, but they have not required so high a
standard that no enterprise could reasonably comply with

it. Of course the courts have founded upon the particular wording of very different statutes, so that what follows describes an emphasis only. But within those limits, the generalisation advanced above is, I submit, sound.

The cases on the application of a false trade description under the Trade Descriptions Act 1968, fairly indicate the propensity of the court. The reading on the odometer of a used car can amount to a trade description under the Act.[57] If it is false, the vendor commits an offence. He can protect himself either by showing that he took reasonable precautions to verify its correctness, or disclaimed reliance on it. In *Naish* v. *Gore*[58] the court dealt with the notion of reasonable precautions. The case would not arise in the same way now since, on the facts, it involved a failure on the part of motor dealers to examine the vehicle log book, a document with which the owner is no longer supplied. The dealers who bought from a firm with which they had dealt before, sold a car before obtaining its log book or verifying the mileage. The magistrates, holding that such a requirement would have been unreasonable, and that the defendant had taken all reasonable precautions, acquitted him. An appeal by the prosecution succeeded. The case is important for the following principles: first that the onus is on the accused to prove either that he took all reasonable precautions or that none could be taken, and secondly that given the prevalence of fraud in this sort of case, the justices should be meticulous in their consideration of the course which the defendant ought to have adopted. O'Connor and Lawson JJ. further state that where the defendant relies on due diligence, he may not be able to invoke section 24(3) which applies to a defect in the content of goods rather than a description applied to them. Nor, Lawson J. states, is a vendor obliged to take a warranty from his supplier. Some legislation embodies a warranty scheme; this statute is not one of them and it should not be introduced by interpretation through the back door.

In such a case as this, the dealer, then, must either take

all reasonable precautions or disclaim reliance on the odometer.[59] The justices must look at the whole field of reasonable precautions.[60] It seems clear that the dealer cannot simply rely on the general appearance of the car as consistent with the odometer roading. Clearly he is put on enquiry where there is an obvious discrepancy between the two.[61] At times, the Divisional Court has enunciated a standard which seems distinctly harsh. Thus in *Simmons* v. *Potter*[62] where the general condition of the car and the odometer reading were consistent and the dealers contacted the first owner of the car and the garage responsible for servicing to learn something about it, but without success, the court held that that was not enough; they should have disclaimed reliance on it. That was an appropriate reasonable precaution and the justices should have considered the whole field of reasonable precautions. But although apparently harsh, the decision is, not unreasonable: where no information can be obtained in such circumstances as these, it is appropriate to smell a rat. In similar vein, it is not surprising that a court refused to allow a dealer to rely on an M.O.T. certificate as evidence of the condition of a car, since the certificate itself says that it cannot be so relied on. The dealer must make his own inspection.[63]

It ought also to be noted that the defendant cannot rely on a disclaimer which he knows to be deceptive. Thus in one case, when the dealer turned back the odometer and then placed a disclaimer notice on each car stating that the mileage shown might not be correct, the disclaimer was held not to be effective because its inaccuracy could not be a mere possibility as suggested by the disclaimer.[64]

The ultimate dependence of defences on particular statutory wording is neatly illustrated by two cases, *Bibby-Cheshire* v. *Golden Wonder Ltd.*,[65] and *Smedleys Ltd.* v. *Breed.*[66] In the former case, a bag of crisps purchased from a retailer was found to be underweight. The manufacturer set up as a defence under s.26(1) of the Weights and Measures Act 1963, that commission of the

offence was due to a mistake or accident or some other
cause beyond his control and that he exercised all due
diligence to prevent its commission. The evidence showed
that no machine was sufficiently accurate to produce no
underweight packages; that tests were made on the
machines and on some packets to check weighing; and
that .0006 per cent. of packets in the weekly ouput could
be underweight. The machines were the best in current
use. In acquitting the defendants, the court held that the
fact that there was an inherent slight tendency to
inaccuracy brought the case within the words "some other
cause beyond his control" in section 26(1) and in addition
all due diligence was used. There was, thus, a clear
indication that the defence is to be administered on
common sense lines, not putting a defendant to an
impossible standard.

In the latter case, *Smedleys Ltd.* v. *Breed*, the House of
Lords refused to interpret legislation so as to produce this
result. The case involved an intrusive caterpillar, found in
a can of Smedley's peas. The defence provided was that it
should be a defence for the accused to prove that the
presence of that matter was an unavoidable consequence
of the process of collection or preparation. The Justices
found that the appellants had taken all reasonable care to
prevent the presence of the caterpillar in the tin. They
nonetheless convicted them and this conviction was
ultimately sustained in the House of Lords. There being
no third party upon whom blame could be shifted, the
appellants sought to argue that the statutory defence
above applied where it was shown that reasonable skill
and diligence had been used to prevent commission of the
offence. Their Lordships refused to gloss the statute thus;
the defence required that the presence of extraneous
matter be an unavoidable consequence of the process of
collection or preparation, a phrase which required that the
defendant both show that he himself exercised every
possible diligence and also that the consequence could
never have been avoided by any other human agency

connected with the process using the requisite degree of
care and diligence. This is harsh enough. Lord Dilhorne
went further; an unavoidable consequence of a process is
something that is bound to result from it. On that basis it
would have to be shown that the presence of at least some
extraneous matter was an inevitable consequence of the
canning process, not a preventable occurrence. No doubt
a canner would rather pay a fine than advance this
argument. Lord Diplock was prepared to concede an
office to due diligence, provided that it could be shown to
have been exercised by everyone engaged in the process,
an onus, surely, virtually impossible to discharge. The
result as this and a later case shows, is to render the
defence almost valueless.[67] Mr. Glazebrook sums the
result up thus:[68]

> "As on previous occasions, the House pointed out
> that there was no obligation on the authorities to
> prosecute—and that the public interest was not
> served by prosecuting—defendants who were clearly
> not at fault, and that if a prosecution was brought the
> courts were free to grant absolute discharges. This
> concession is unlikely to satisfy the jurist, and serves
> the consumer only on the assumption, which may be
> well-founded, that officers responsible for the en-
> forcement of this legislation demand higher standards
> of care if a trader is to escape prosecution than the
> courts do if he is to escape a conviction grounded on
> his failure to disprove negligence."

It is difficult to see how this latter assumption corresponds
to the facts of this case, which seems anomalous in the
light of the general approach adopted by the court.
Undoubtedly it is right in the interests of consumer
protection to insist on a high standard of reasonable care,
but the result of *Smedleys Ltd.* v. *Breed* is virtually to
impose upon the manufacturer an insurer's liability. The
alternative, which is presumably to contend that the entry
of a foreign substance into tinned goods is, truly,

inevitable, is hardly likely to appeal to a food processing company.

In respect of the third party element of such defences, the courts have endeavoured to work out who may and who may not be said to be truly independent of the defendant for the purpose. The problem arises under s.24 of the Trade Descriptions Act 1968, for example. Because that provision speaks of due diligence and reasonable care by a defendant to ensure that an offence will not be committed by him or by any person under his control, he cannot simply set up as a defence that the infraction was due to the act or default of such a person.[69] He must go further, to show that he created and operated a suitable system of control.

The principles were elaborated in *Tesco Supermarkets Ltd.* v. *Nattrass.*[70] An information was laid against the defendants for offering to supply goods to which a false trade description concerning price was applied, contrary to s.11(2) of the Trade Descriptions Act 1968. Their defence was that the act or default was due to "another person", their manager, and that they had used all due diligence to secure compliance with the provisions in question. The manager was adequately inspected and trained, there was an elaborate system of supervision to ensure that the shops were managed properly, and inspections were regularly carried out. Their Lordships held that the company could rely on the due diligence defence, and could set up the conduct of the manager as the act or default of a third person. In the first place the manager was not to be regarded as the *alter ego* of the company, and his acts could not therefore be attributed to the company as acts personal to it. Secondly, an employer can defend himself by showing due diligence and may set up the act or default of an employee as that of another person. The defence is intended to be available to employers. But, thirdly, the company must adopt a precautionary system and exercise due diligence in its operation. This is a non-delegable duty and had not been delegated to the manager who was being directed by the company in these matters. As Lord Morris states:[71]

> "He was a person under the control of the company and on the assumption that there could be proceedings against him, the company would by section 24(1)(*b*) be absolved if the company had taken all proper steps to avoid the commission of an offence by him. To make the company automatically liable for an offence committed by him would be to ignore the subsection."

The critical questions, then, are of system and operation. Yet this reasoning does not seem to have been applied to the very similar provisions of s.26(1) of the Weights and Measures Act 1963 where it has been held that the defence cannot operate where the actual offender is under the defendant's control.[72] These decisions would seem to be inconsistent with *Tesco Supermarkets Ltd.* v. *Nattrass* and of no authority.[73]

A number of miscellaneous cases also concern the integrity of such defences. This account makes no pretence to completeness, but the following are important. First, the third party procedure can be very wide. Under s.113 of the Food and Drugs Act 1955, a third party to whose act or default an infraction is due need not be directly concerned in the provision of food; it is enough if a sale in contravention is due to his act or default, as where he left cleaning solution in such a location that the proprietor sold it as lemonade.[74] Secondly, where the matter sought to be raised is the act or default of another person, the defendant must rely on those words and give the necessary notice. He may not, for example, seek to rely on such an act as a defence of mistaken reliance, so denying the prosecution the opportunity of considering whether or not to bring proceedings against the person directly involved.[75] Each person accused, whether directly or by third party procedure may, however, bring another before the court as the actual offender, and the conduct of a whole chain of persons may thus be placed in issue.[76] Because the offence of applying a false trade description is one of strict liability, a partner may be liable for the act of application even though he did not do so personally.[77] Furthermore, courts must consider, in working the machinery, whether offences are connected or independent.[78] Thus dealers who purchased a car and sold it by auction where it was bought by the defendant no disclaimer of mileage on the odometer having been then made, were not persons to whose act or default defendant's later sale of the car in contravention of the Trades Description Act 1968, could be attributed.[79]

A judicial combination of strictness and common sense is again shown by decisions on the defence of reliance upon a warranty. In *Rochdale Metropolitan Borough Council* v. *F.M.C. (Meat) Ltd.*,[80] the court holds that a brand name in an invoice can amount to a written warranty under s.115 of the Food and Drugs Act 1955, that the food was fit for human consumption. But of course the accused has to establish a series of other matters under the section, for example that he had no reason to believe that the substance could not lawfully be sold, that the article was in the same state as when he purchased it, and that the person giving the warranty can be proceeded against, either for giving a false warranty or for selling food unfit for human consumption. The court expressly notes first that there is a need to give reasonable breadth to due diligence defences so as to avoid convicting persons not at fault, and secondly to have regard to contemporary market practice where frequently the trade name of an item of food is the best guarantee of its quality.

Conclusions

We have seen that it is uncertain to what extent a general common law defence of due diligence can be raised to crimes of strict liability and therefore to many crimes of vicarious liability as well. There are areas of activity which are not covered by statutory defences. In respect of many activities, particularly in relation to public health and consumer safety and standards such defences do exist. They tend to follow roughly standardised forms, are particular in their address, and enable persons and companies who show that they have complied with their exacting requirements to avoid conviction. Generally speaking, the courts have applied them strictly but sensibly, certain exceptions apart. Much, therefore, of the debate concerning the supposed rigour of the law and the absence of any recognition of a fault principle is beside the point. To a marked extent Parliament has supplied the omission of the courts and, indeed, has done so ever since the Merchandise Marks Act 1887. Certainly it can be argued that this is a superior method to that of judicial legislation, and it is not clear that all legislative failures to provide such a defence represent lacunae which, the courts ought to fill.

Not all scholars would agree with this assessment. No one considers that the existing system of defences is perfect. Professor Hogan contends that the Law Commission should have come out in favour of a general no negligence defence.[81] He argues, furthermore, that serious offences, for example those under the Misuse of Drugs Act 1971, should not be offences of negligence. Two issues arise. The first concerns the mental element which should be insisted upon in crimes where the maximum penalty is severe. That issue is discussed in the final chapter. The other issue, pertinent here, concerns whether a general defence, in addition to specific defences, should be enacted into law. There seems no reason why it should not be, provided first that it does not undercut specific statutory schemes which provide limited defences. Such limitations are usually imposed for defensible reasons of public policy. Secondly, one would have to accept, unless offences in future to specify with precision the *mens rea* required, that the existence of such a defence might lead courts to sweep into the net of strict liability, offences which otherwise might be regarded as requiring *mens rea*. Thirdly, such a defence would be defective unless it were to extend to some mistakes of law. Modern regulatory legislation is undeniably complicated and it seems unjust that a person cannot rely on advice, for example of a lawyer or of an official agency, and plead that advice as a defence to a charge concerning a regulatory offence.[82] Finally it would be necessary to exclude from the defence cases where it really does seem necessary to make the accused absolutely liable as in the case of moving traffic offences.

NOTES

[1] As noted above, the notion that the absence of *mens rea* words merely shifted the burden of proof to the defendant to prove no fault, has been rejected.

[2] Criminal Law Act 1977, s.58.

[3] [1980] 1 W.L.R. 823.

[4] [1971] 3 All E.R. 220.

[5] (1966) 50 Cr.App.R. 266.

[6] [1961] 2 Q.B. 205; see also *Reg.* v. *Atkinson* [1970] R.T.R. 265.

[7] [1952] 2 Q.B. 668.

[8] [1967] 1 Q.B. 227.

[9] [1980] N.Z.L.R. 51.

[10] *Haynes* v. *Swain* [1975] R.T.R. 40.

[11] [1975] Crim.L.R. 521.

[12] *R.* v. *Howells* [1977] Q.B. 614, and see M. Bowen, D. Fox and A. Khan, "Strict Liability Offences: How Strict", (1979) 123 S.J. 72.

[13] [1973] R.T.R. 202.

[14] [1970] A.C. 132 at p. 163.

[15] (1943) 67 C.L.R. 536; for a full consideration, see C. Howard, *Strict Responsibility* (1963) pp. 99–112.

[16] (1943) 67 C.L.R. 536 at p. 540.

[17] See, for a formulation, *Reg. ex rel Carswell* v. *City of Sault St. Marie* [1978] 2 S.C.R. 1299.

[18] *Woolmington* v. *D.P.P.* [1935] A.C. 462.

[19] [1975] 2 W.L.R. 923.

[20] *Ibid.* at pp. 935–36; the entire passage is confused, for Lord Cross

also speaks in the same breath of an offence which is absolute on the face of it.

[21] (1889) 23 Q.B.D. 168.

[22] [1975] 2 W.L.R. 937H.

[23] (1974) 9 S.A.S.R. 495.

[24] See Fish Conservation Act 1967, s.9; Import of Live Fish (England and Wales) Act 1980, s.3.

[25] See Sess. 1973–74, 348, H.L. Deb., col. 1430. The Bill lapsed on the dissolution of Parliament in 1974.

[26] Sess. 1974, Stg. Cttee. A., Control of Pollution Bill (Lords) cols. 53–4.

[27] The influence of such views can be seen in the debates on the Clean Air Bill, 1956. See for example Sess. 545 H.C. Deb. (Vth Ser.) , cols. 1327–8, and Vol. 55I H.C. Deb (Vth Ser.), cols. 91, 127, 143 and 146. The question concerned the strictness with which defences were to be drafted and Members were certainly aware of the defects of a widely drafted defence under previous legislation.

[28] Poisons Act 1972, s.8(2) (*a*) and (*b*).

[29] Dumping At Sea Act 1974, s.1(7); a similar defence structure applies to employees and to persons who act on the advice of others. Interestingly, in both cases, the accused must prove that he took all such steps as were reasonably open to him to ensure that no offence would be committed: *ibid.* s.1(8).

[30] Slaughterhouses Act 1974, s.39(3).

[31] Road Traffic Regulation Act 1967, s.79.

[32] "Zebra" Pedestrian Crossings Regulation, S.I. 1971, No.1524; "Pelican" Pedestrian Crossing Regulations and General Directions, S.I. 1969 No.888, reg. l2.

[33] *The Times* L.R., 17 October, 1981.

[34] [1972] 1 All E.R. 1037.

[35] (1964) 27 M.L.R. 98.

[36] Deposit of Poisonous Wastes Act 1972, s.1(6)(*a*)(i).

[37] *e.g.* International Carriage of Perishable Foodstuffs Act 1976, s.7(3).

[38] Weights and Measures Act 1963, s.16(2)(*a*) and (*b*).

[39] *Ibid.* s.25(1)(*a*)–(*d*).

[40] *Ibid.* s.25(4).

[41] *Ibid.* s.25(6).

[42] *Ibid.* s.26(1)(*a*) and (*b*).

[43] *Ibid.* s.26(2).

[44] *Ibid.* s.26(2), and (3).

[45] *Ibid.* s.27(1).

[46] *Ibid.* s.27(1)(*b*); for the procedural rights of the third party, see s.27(2).

[47] *Oxo Ltd.* v. *Chappell and Turner* [1966] 3 All E.R. 168.

[48] *Simmonds* v. *London Central Meat Co. Ltd.* [1958] Crim.L.R. 47.

⁴⁹ Bell and O' Keefe, *Sale of Food and Drugs* (14 ed., 1968), p. 222 notes that the machinery which is used by accused both against their employees and their suppliers gives rise to difficulties.

⁵⁰ *Ibid.* s.27(4).

⁵¹ *Ibid.* s.27(3).

⁵² Weights and Measures Act 1979, ss.1 and 3.

⁵³ See, for background, *Final Report of the Committee on Consumer Protection*, 1962, Cmnd. 1781; the references to legislation refer to the since repealed Merchandise Marks Act 1881.

⁵⁴ Fair Trading Act 1973, ss.25(3) and 121(1): see also the Banking Act 1979, s.41(*a*).

⁵⁵ Consumer Credit Act 1974, s.168 (but the offences seem cast in terms which permit the party responsible to be convicted anyway).

⁵⁶ Transport Act 1980, ss.42(2) and (3).

⁵⁷ *Stainthorpe* v. *Bailey* [1979] Crim.L.R. 677.

⁵⁸ [1971] 3 All E.R. 737.

⁵⁹ *Stainthorpe* v. *Bailey, supra.* In similar vein, dealing with reliance on M.O.T. certificates, see *Baker* v. *Hargreaves* [1981] Crim.L.R. 262.

⁶⁰ *Sherratt* v. *Gerald's The American Jewellers Ltd.* (1970) 68 L.G.R. 256.

⁶¹ *Lewis* v. *Maloney* [1977] Crim.L.R. 436, D.C.

⁶² [1975] R.T.R. 347.

⁶³ *Baker* v. *Hargreaves* [1981] Crim.L.R. 262.

⁶⁴ *Reg.* v. *King* [1979] Crim.L.R. 122.

⁶⁵ [1972] 1 W.L.R. 1487.

⁶⁶ [1974] A.C. 839.

⁶⁷ *Greater Manchester Council* v. *Lockwood Foods Ltd.* [1979] Crim.L.R. 593.

⁶⁸ [1974] A.S.C.L. 636.

⁶⁹ *Hall* v. *Farmer* [1970] 1 W.L.R. 766; *Pickover* v. *Smith* [1975] Crim.L.R. 529.

⁷⁰ [1972] A.C. 153.

⁷¹ *Ibid.* at p. 180.

⁷² *Pickover* v. *Smith* [1975] Crim.L.R. 529; *Hall* v. *Farmer* [1970] 1 W.L.R. 366.

⁷³ Similarly, *Beckett* v. *Kingston Bros. (Butchers) Ltd.* [1970] 1 Q.B. 606 would seem to be overruled.

⁷⁴ *Meah* v. *Roberts* [1977] 1 W.L.R. 1187.

⁷⁵ *Birkenhead and District Cooperative Society Ltd.* v. *Roberts* [1970] 1 W.L.R. 1497.

⁷⁶ *British Fermentation Products Ltd.* v. *British Italian Trading Co. Ltd.* [1942] 2 K.B. 145.

⁷⁷ *Clode* v. *Barnes* [1974] 1 W.L.R. 544.

⁷⁸ *Coupe* v. *Guyett* [1973] 1 W.L.R. 669.

⁷⁹ *Tarleton Engineering Co. Ltd.* v. *Nattrass* [1973] 1 W.L.R. 1261.

⁸⁰ [1980] 2 All E.R. 303.

[81] B. Hogan, "Strict Liability" [1978] Crim.L.R. 593.

[82] A. J. Ashworth, "Excusable Mistake of Law" [1974] Crim.L.R. 652 at pp. 657 ff.; G. P. Fletcher, *Rethinking Criminal Law* (1978), pp. 755–758.

Chapter 5

ENFORCEMENT OF THE LAW

It is in respect of enforcement that the status of the offences which we have been considering, as administrative criminal law, most clearly appears. Enforcement by no means always depends primarily upon the clumsy instrument of the criminal law. The criminal law as a means of controlling the activities of enterprises in particular suffers from deficiencies and defects which enforcement authorities have sought to overcome or mitigate, virtually from the dawn of regulation. In part, there is a problem that sentence in a given case, unless the accused has past convictions, is unlikely to mark sufficiently the inherent gravity of his or its conduct, especially where the accused has a history of non-compliance with social legislation, but has never been convicted so that the history is known only to administrators. More fundamentally, there is the obvious problem that even with the aid of doctrines of strict and vicarious liability, the state cannot deploy enough enforcement personnel to enforce its rules comprehensively. There are bound to be few prosecutions, and, inevitably, regulators will seek to establish cooperation between themselves and the firms whose activities they regulate; but this could hardly be fostered under a regime of routine prosecution for infractions. Partnership, not bullying, has been the desired mode. Thus it is that cooperation, and ultimately administrative measures of control, have been the dominant modes of enforcement of much regulatory legislation. And while in some instances, of which marine pollution is a striking example, society has had to rely on the threat of heavy fines as a primary weapon through the impossibility of securing compliance otherwise, a softer approach has been characteristic of enforcement elsewhere.[1]

Prosecutorial discretion bulks large in the practical administration of the law. It has been the subject of at least four major studies, the thrust of which however was to examine the relationship between prosecution policies and the fault principle.[2] This is an interesting aspect of the problem, no doubt, but it is only an aspect of it. Of course the spectacle of courts insisting upon discretion to prosecute as a safeguard against unmeritorious prosecution is a familiar and salutary one. There is no point in prosecuting where the violation is merely technical, where there really is no fault, and where a conviction is unlikely to produce any useful result. But, at the risk of anticipating the argument, one cannot readily assume that because studies show that prosecutions are not commenced unless the offender was at fault, blamelessness is therefore adequately catered for by prosecutorial discretion. In the first place, there can be no agreed abstract meaning to be given to fault; it needs to be assessed in relation to particular fact situations and to the law applicable to them. Secondly, it by no means follows even so, that whether there is fault in a particular situation would be generally agreed, or whether, if it were, that fault would be such as all persons would agree sought to serve as a justification for prosecution. As an example, we may take *Alphacell Ltd.* v. *Woodward*.[3] It happens that Viscount Dilhorne, who participated in that judgment, believed that the company was at fault, not indeed because it could be shown to have been privy to the acutual discharge, but because the system was installed in such a place that a forbidden overflow was bound to occur unless it could be successfully prevented.[4] Now whether this amounted to fault at all cannot be pursued here; one would have to know whether in fact the plant could have been sited elsewhere and whether and what environmental and planning considerations were raised and pursued. But, equally, even if the company were at fault in that respect, it is not necessarily the case that that fault was the relevant question whether liability should be imposed. The right criterion might well have been fault in the actual operation of the system once installed. This is not to argue that Viscount Dilhorne was wrong, but simply that even conceding the presence of fault, it may not apply to a stage in the operations where all would agree that it ought to be considered in the decision to prosecute. A third and obvious point is that considerations of fault may be catered for, largely or exclusively, by affirmative defences of a comprehensive and minutely expressed character. In respect of pollution, incidentally, such defences were regarded with some considerable suspicion; the operation of fault was thought, by many spokesmen, but not by the Law Commission, to be best left to discretion, lest unscrupulous enterprises brought themselves, wrongly, within it by a mere apparent compliance with its terms.[5]

Faced with difficult practical problems of enforcement regulatory bodies relied to a great extent on cooperation with industry. This, of course, requires a good deal of mutual accommodation. Authorities must consider to what extent businesses can be relied upon to rectify faults. They must concentrate their resources upon the worst offenders. Sometimes their resources are so slender that enforcement becomes lax.

Historically, cooperative enforcement through information, exhortation and warnings was adopted in respect of food and drugs, pollution, and factories legislation. In respect of food and drugs, Dr. Paulus notes that strict liability provisions were not used indiscriminately to punish offenders who might well be innocent. The primary machinery for enforcement was provided by such steps as informal sampling, inspection of premises, verbal admonitions, advice, official cautions, and the speedy withdrawal of suspected toxic substances. These were felt by enforcers to be more effectual than court proceedings and fines in preventing adulterations and accidental poisonings. Thus, she states:[6]

" . . . the accommodations between the controllers and the controllees resulting from changing economic conditions, business practices and technological innovations worked primarily on the *preventive* level; only when this phase of the control process was ineffectual or inadequate was the actual legal machinery based on the *detection* of law-breaking involved. The legal process then became a punishing and deterrent one—punishing for a particular recalcitrant law-breaker, and deterring for possible others."

Indeed, there was a trend towards industry support for enforcement in order to equalise the conditions of competition, and pressure by small merchants for more adequate controls against manufacturers and processors who were not adequately controlled by proceedings against retailers. But the degree of success enjoyed in the fight against adulteration does reflect that a vigorous enforcement policy was followed.

Paulus' study is confirmed in general terms by that of Smith and Pearson.[7] Studies carried out for the Law Reform Commission of Canada also testify to the use of a principled discretion.[8] That inquiry was into the exercise of discretion in offences of false advertising, weights and measures and food and drugs. In each discretion was exercised, though most strongly so in relation to false advertising. Prosecution was brought where there was a previous history of complaints against the enterprise, or its alleged mistake was not reasonable, or the excuse given was too tortuous to be believable, or it was desired to test the matter before the court. Other factors, applicable to much crime, such as delay in bringing proceedings, were also relevant. Readiness of the enterprise to make redress to the victim was regarded as of great importance. The enforcing Department, as with its English counterparts, considered it better to protect the consumer by cooperation with enterprises than by repressive enforcement. In respect of the other offences, enforced by different agencies, discretion was more structured and less frequently exercised. A well developed administrative scheme of warning notices, injunctions and prosecutions applies, with certain infractions such as the sale of dangerous products or misclassification of products leading to prosecution. *In rem* measures such as the seizure or sealing up of equipment are also used, as they are in such regulation in Britain. But, once again, inspectors look to a course of conduct, rather than an isolated error, in determining whether to prosecute. Once again, there is a strong emphasis on cooperative enforcement.

The same degree of success was not achieved in respect of pollution. Gunningham argues that the Alkali Inspectorate enforces standards as a self-conceived partner of industry, not as an independent judge, and is caught between serving the industry and the public.[9] Persuasion and cooperation are preferred to prosecution which is only used where the firm is thought to be flouting the law. The prevalence of warnings and the relative absence of convictions is attested to in Parlimentary debates on pollution. Penalties, are, he says too low, and defences too permissive. The problem of competitive disadvantage has also been raised; that those industrialists who installed efficient filtration machinery would suffer a cost disadvantage by comparison with their competitors.[10] Enforcement cannot have been facilitated by the fact that municipalities also were often badly at fault as polluters because of their financial inability to provide efficient filtration plants.[11] Central government played its part too. McLoughlin notes that when the Rivers (Prevention of Pollution) Act 1951 was passed, the Minister issued a circular which emphasised the requirements of industry and encouraged "wise and patient administration by river boards, working in close touch with local authorities and industry". River boards responded to this, and attempted to enforce the law by persuasion. McLoughlin states:[12]

> "Most would prosecute only when a breach: of consent conditions had caused serious damage, or had been wilfull, or the result of gross negligence, or

where there had been persistent breaches in the face of warnings."

There does, certainly, appear to be substance to some of the criticism made. Cooperation can no doubt become toothlessness. In the debates on the Control of Pollution Bill 1974, speakers contended that the Inspectorate were cosying along firms rather than relying on prosecutions. While no one wanted to prosecute every firm which failed to come up to the mark, a figure of 14 prosecutions since 1920 was thought to be unduly low.[13] It was doubts concerning the enforeability of legislation which led speakers to argue against the establishment of due diligence defences. The debate is itself a trifle muddled on the point; some strange assertions about the effect of "causing" on *mens rea* appeared—it was thought always to require it.[14] Certainly it was not assumed that criminal and even injunctive proceedings would become common modes of recourse. Enforcers, in their discretion would, as always, rely on inspection, persuasion and negotiation.

Pollution control is interesting in another aspect as well. Control is in fact very widely based, and criminal proceedings take their place with a bundle of other legal controls.[15] Under the Water Act 1973, the Secretaries of State for the Environment and for Agriculture, Fisheries and Food are obliged to promote a national policy for water in England and Wales, including the restoration and wholesomeness of rivers and other inland water. There are a wide range of administrative measures which apply to control various forms of pollution. These include plannning permissions, permissions prior to carrying out work involving the discharge of effluent into sewers and rivers, chimney heights and dust and grit controls under the Clean Air Acts, and administrative controls under the Alkali Act 1906 which extends to a wide range of manufacturing activities. Administrative sanctions include the revocation or modification of a planning permission or a discontinuance order requiring removal of a building or works the enforcement of planning control by requiring removal of unauthorised development or discontinued uses, enforcement and stop notices under the Public Health Acts, and local authority powers to close or restrict the use of water from a polluted source of supply. There is thus no shortage of administrative controls which can be wielded by administrators whether in conjunction with criminal provisions or not. This is a chracteristic mix which applies also, as we will see, under modern factory legislation.

This does not mean that the authorities avoid prosecution in all cases of pollution. In some, enforcement appears to be quite strict. Thus it has been said that harbour authorities are not reluctant to prosecute.[16] If a conviction seems likely, prosecutions are withheld only both where the pollution and blameworthiness are minimal. Brown states:[17]

> "Substantial pollution (no matter how good a plea in mitigation may be put forward) or substantial negligence (notwithstanding the extent of the spill) usually lead to prosecution."

It seems clear that pollution has been less successfully tackled overall than has food and drug adulteration. This is probably attributable first to the fact that the enforcement problems are more intractable in this area. For example, there are obvious problems associated with pollution by foreign owned ships. Officers of river boards endeavoured to control pollution by discussing with firms the treatment processes which the latter used, so that they could see whether reasonable efforts were being made to comply with consent conditions. Alkali inspectors have long acted like this, but, McLoughlin concludes, river boards faced the problem that they lacked enough men with scientific and technical skills to operate that form of control efficiently in all cases. They were competent to advise and persuade small firms, but "in large industrial complexes such as petro-chemical plants they did not have the expertise to know what could be expected or reasonably demanded."[18] Water authorities, too, are themselves polluters when discharging their sewage disposal functions. There are also different authorities dealing with the many manifestations of pollution. This fragmentation of function cannot, surely, be helpful. This unhappy record does not establish that non-penal strategies and methods of enforcement are inherently unsatisfactory. Nor do low levels of fines necessarily demonstrate that courts are unwilling to enforce legislation adequately. In relation to marine pollution, Brown points out that most infractions are not the result of a deliberate disregard of good practice by shipowners, but arise from an employee's error of judgment, which seems to indicate that non-penal methods of control through exhortation, information and the like work, and secondly that in serious cases magistrates do in fact impose high fines.

Finally, we may cite the use of discretion under the Factories Acts, an area particularly well documented thanks to the work of the Law Commission and Dr. Carson. The latter has written that assiduous efforts to attempt to make regulation a reality collided with other intransigent forces embedded in the social organisation of factory production in the early 19th century and that this culminated in ambiguity becoming the salient feature of factory crime. One of the first problems confronting the inspectors after 1836:[19]

" . . . was the not uncommon one of demonstrating to those whom they supervised that their enforcement policy was not arbitrary or essentially unjust."

Their consistent strategy, which Carson argues became an institutionalised feature of factory inspection, was to prosecute only where the enterprise in question apparently intended to flout the law. The historical vicissitudes of the fault principle need not detain us here. We should, however, note Carson's argument that violations were the work, not of a few bad offenders, but of social forces; of

the result of economic pressures coupled with orthodox
assumptions about the necessary interdependence of
labour, capital investment, and costs. Violations were, he
argues, not a concentrated evil, but a pervasive one.[20] The
criminals involved were often the representatives of a
respectable and politically powerful class. And so Inspectors sought to enforce the law by combining firmness with
conciliation; to advise rather than police, with prosecution
utilised as a last resort. According to Carson, the pattern
of factory law enforcement was thus set at an early stage,
and the ambiguity of factory crime established.

Carson's earlier study into the enforcement of the
Factories Act, and that of the Law Commission indicated
that considerable reliance was placed on warnings and
advice, and prosecution decisions tended to reflect
whether previous instructions and warnings had in fact
been given to the prospective accused.[21] Fault in the
nature of blatant non-compliance with the statute,
together with the inspectors' store of knowledge about
particular firms, was of considerable importance in determining what mode enforcement would take. These views
were guided also by the criteria outlined in due diligence
defences; indeed, Carson argues that what ought to be
emphasised is the likely impact of such a defence upon the
agents of law enforcement rather than its accessibility and
attractiveness to morally blameless offenders. The dominant attitude of the factory inspectorate was, however,
that its function was not simply or primarily to apprehend
or punish offenders, but rather to secure compliance with
the law and to ensure that occupiers adhered to the
highest standards which might reasonably be expected at
any time. Prosecution based on previous impressions and
warnings were, he concluded, often instituted in order to
cause management to rectify a situation, rather than to
inflict punishment. The Law Commission study reached
very similar conclusions; primary reliance was placed on
an extended system of cautioning with a decision to
prosecute being taken where previous advice was ignored,

or many matters needed rectification, or a serious injury had resulted. Curiously, given their general remedial function, the inspectors made little use of procedures *in rem* such as enforcement and closure orders.[22]

But, while we may conclude that over a wide area of regulatory crime, structured discretion ensures both that fault will be catered for adequately, and that prosecutions will not be a common mode of enforcement, the same cannot be said of every strict liability offence.[23] For example, moving vehicle offences are very often, indeed in some areas generally prosecuted, and this has been the case for a very long time. There is a considerable variation in practice between police areas; Halnan noted that in the Metropolitan police area there were 39 prosecutions to each warning, in Dyfed-Powys the figure was 2.21–1, with a national average of 7.34 prosecutions to each warning.[24] The emphasis certainly differs from that in the topics just mentioned. Indeed, in the debates on the Road Traffic Act 1962, the policy was said to be that most forces would lay all proper charges which arise from a moving traffic offence.[25] This is no doubt inevitable, given that, save where he has previously been convicted, the police have not been aware of the way in which a particular motorist behaved and have not had the opportunity to judge his compliance with the road traffic acts that an inspector would have of a factory.

The problem of ensuring effective punishment for the recidivist road traffic offender is, of course, ensured by the totting up and disqualification procedure.[26] It was clear from a very early period that fines alone were unlikely to provide a sufficient safeguard in the public interest, and that a universal licensing and disqualification system would be required.[27] The Royal Commission on Transport of 1929 expressly drew attention to the deficiences of fines as a deterrent, and insisted both that the available range of disqualifications be extended and that persons who drove while disqualified should be imprisoned.[28] The need for ample powers of disqualification has of course been met, and is exercised with some rigour as those who seek to show that they have special reasons for not being disqualified are aware.[29]

We have, so far, stressed the findings of studies concerning the past enforcement of administrative criminal law We may now turn, by way of example, to the scheme of enforcement created by the Health and Safety at Work Act 1974, which is the successor to earlier Factories legislation.[30] Critical of the inhibitions to effective enforcement outlined by the research findings alluded to above, the Robens Report recommended a new approach which buttressed exhortations and warnings by more severe measures against persons who failed to obey the law.[31] Parliament, therefore, passed the Health and Safety at Work Act 1974, the most important characteristics of which are the following:

(1) the creation of a Health and Safety Executive vested with regulatory responsibilities in respect of health, safety and conditions of work in factories;

(2) the vesting of power in the executive to appoint inspectors or to adopt those already employed by local authorities;

(3) the bestowal upon inspectors of extended powers of coercion, both positive and negative. Among the positive powers are those of ordering the rectification of practices dangerous to health and safety. Among the positive powers are those of ordering the rectification of practices dangerous to health and safety; among the negative powers are those of ordering that dangerous practices cease. Inspectors are empowered to seize articles which pose an immediate danger. The role of the criminal law is essentially the supplementary one of punishing a failure to implement recommendations made by the inspectors.

The annual reports of the Health and Safety Commission, chronicling its activities and those of the Health and Safety Executive, indicate that these policies are being faithfully observed. The accent is not upon prosecution; there is, instead, a tendency to use other formal procedures such as improvement and prohibition notices, as well as information and exhortation. The Commission, in its report for 1977–78 thus states:[32]

"The term 'enforcement' does not only mean taking punitive action, but covers the whole range of procedures adopted by inspectorates to ensure employers are aware of and comply with their responsibilities under health and safety legislation. The inspectors' main concern is not to identify particular breaches of health and safety legislation so that they can prosecute the offender, but to ensure that management recognises its responsibilities for the control of hazards, to provide an effective policy for health and safety, proper organisation and carry it out and arrangements to ensure safe systems of work and to check the results regularly."

The Commission, accordingly, insists that enforcement activities cannot be measured simply by the volume of prosecutions. It lays stress on visiting and inspections, whilst admitting that with some 500,000 to 600,000 premises subject to the Act, not all can be visited with any regularity. It concentrates its resources on scrutinising premises which are assessed on grounds of intrinsic hazard, previously observed standards, and quality of management controls. In a word, it clearly engages in targeting. Its powers to issue improvement and prohibition notices are seen as prophylactic or protective rather than punitive measures. It prefers to proceed on the basis of agreement in raising levels of health in the workplace, health and safety awareness, and in encouraging a more positive approach to combating hazards.[33]

Some cases are regarded as right for prosecution. Where there is a risk of serious personal injury, a prohibition notice will issue. Where the offender has flouted the law in a flagrant manner, the authority will

prosecute. In 1977, 6,233 improvement notices were
issued, 2,666 prohibition notices were issued and 1600
prosecutions were commenced. The figures for 1976–77
show 5,044 improvement notices, 1778 immediate and 512
deferred prohibition notices and 1,200 prosecutions.[34]
Later figures show the same emphasis.[35] Furthermore,
fines for indictable cases have been raised to £1,000 by the
Criminal Law Act 1977, a step welcomed by the Health
and Safety Commission not because success is measurable
in terms of successful prosecutions, but because:[36]

> " . . . where serious offences often resulting in death
> or serious injury are punished with a paltry fine, this
> devalues the work of all those who are making real
> efforts to reduce occupational hazards."

The following conclusions can be drawn from the
experience of enforcement of legislation pertaining to
health and safety in the workplace. First, that the powers
to issue improvement and prohibition notices are useful.
They afford a speedy and direct method of dealing with
situations which involve a risk to health and safety.
Secondly, the existence of such procedures with a criminal
sanction for breach eases the task of bringing criminal
proceedings, since it is now only necessary to prove
non-compliance with the notices, rather than a specific
contravention of the standards embodied in the legislation. Thirdly, the use of the criminal sanction is a last
resort; it is a buttress, but it is not a primary tool of
enforcement. In effect, there has been a change in formal
emphasis from a stress upon the criminal law to a stress
upon administrative procedures. It would, however, be
wrong to think that the system has entirely altered. The
notion of co-operation as a prime method of regulation, of
securing compliance with standards, is traditional and
continues. These conclusions are of course tentative. We
await empirical research into the practical working of
these new procedures, and the growth of a body of
evaluating literature.

Similar generalisations apply, as we have noted, in the field of pollution control. A wide range of administrative powers exists in respect of various forms of pollution.[37] These carry powers to prosecute for offences, some of which carry condign penalties. Yet, as we have noted, it is clear that here also, the accent is on co-operation in prevention rather than on prosecution. Reports of the statutory water authorities do, for example, mention prosecutions in flagrant cases, some of which appear to have produced the desired effect, but the numbers are not great and it is clear that the authorities prefer to reserve prosecutions for cases where the firms involved are careless, irresponsible or unwilling to cooperate.[38] This is consistent with the emphasis which has always applied in these matters. The same may be said of prosecutions for air pollution.[39]

There are other instances of the use of administrative procedures to regulate conduct which formerly seems to have been dealt with largely by the criminal law. Consumer protection is an example. There, of course, the criminal law is still extensively used; much of the applicable legislation is expressed to be enforceable under criminal penalties, but there are obvious harbingers of change.[40] In some instances, for example, contractual terms are made invalid civilly.[41] The most striking development is the creation of the Office of Fair Trading under the Fair Trading Act 1974, in some respects similar to United States regulatory agencies in that the Director-General of Fair Trading has quasi-legislative powers as well as powers of enforcement. His powers of enforcement include the power to seek a written assurance from a trader who has persisted in a course of conduct detrimental to the interests of consumers and has disregarded his obligations under the civil or criminal law, that he will refrain from continuing his course of conduct. Where a trader, having given such an assurance fails to abide by it, the Director-General can seek an order from the court requiring him to refrain from conduct specified in the assurance. Breach of a court order, once made, amounts to contempt of court which may in the case of an individual be punished by imprisonment, but which in the ordinary case would no doubt be fined. The emphasis is clearly the same as that which applies to the enforcement of health and safety, or pollution, legislation.

It is, perhaps, strange that tendencies which have long been evident in English administrative law have not been discussed in those terms. Academic accounts have tended to discuss the phenomenon of strict liability while practitioners' works, understandably, look to the rules which govern particular regulated topics. Yet the law as well as the practice evidences an emphasis on administrative regulation including the evolution of standards. It seems to be in such areas as marine pollution which pose particular problems of enforcement for any agency including the problems of securing international action that stringently punished criminal offences appear to be the most prominent of the recourses for control. For example, the Prevention of Oil Pollution Act 1971 imposed a maximum fine of £50,000 on summary conviction and an unlimited fine on indictment. Even so, the available defences told the accused what steps had to be taken in order to avoid conviction, including notification so that prompt remedial action could be taken. But generally, enforcement legislation both envisages and to a marked extent structures discretion. To some extent this has been true since the Clauses Acts of the mid-nineteenth century, although it becomes more obvious now.

NOTES

[1] See Merchant Shipping Oil Pollution Bill (Lords), Standing Committee E, Sess. 1970–71 , vol. IV.

[2] Law Commission, Working Paper No.30. *Strict liability and the Factories Act*; Smith and Pearson, "The Value of Strict Liability", [1969]

Crim.L.R. 5; W. G. Carson, "Some Sociological Aspects of Strict Liability and the Enforcement of Factory Legislation" (1970) 33 M.L.R. 396; Law Reform Commission of Canada, *Studies on Strict Liability* (1974).

[3] [1972] A.C. 824.

[4] Sess. 1973–74, 348 H.L. Deb. (Vth Ser.), col. 1430.

[5] *E.g.* see Control of Pollution Bill (Lords) 1974, H.C. Standing Committee F, cols. 53–4.

[6] I. Paulus, *The Search for Pure Food: A Sociology of Legislation in Britain* (1974), p. 103.

[7] M. Smith and A. Pearson, "The Value of Strict Liability", [1969] Crim.L.R. 5.

[8] Law Reform Commission of Canada, *Studies in Strict Liability* (1974).

[9] N. Gunningham, *Pollution, Social Interest and the Law* (1974).

[10] Sess. 1965–66, 545 H.C. Deb. (Vth Ser.), col. 91.

[11] G. H. Newsom Q.C., "River pollution and the Law", (1971) 2 Otago L. Rev. 381; for a comparable Canadian study, see P. Anisman, "Water Pollution Control in Ontario", (1972) 5 O.H.L.J. 342.

[12] J. McLoughlin, *The Law and Practice Relating to Pollution Control in the United Kingdom*, (1976) p. 111.

[13] Sess. 875 H.C. Deb. (Vth Ser.), cols. 122–3.

[14] Sess. 877 H.C. Deb. (Vth Ser.), col. 931.

[15] See further, J. McLoughlin, *op. cit.*, and J. A. Beale, *The Contribution of Criminal Law to the Protection of the Environment*, European Committee on Crime Problems, Council of Europe, Strasbourg, 1974.

[16] R. A. Brown, "Enforcement of Oil Pollution Legislation: A Practitioner's View", (1976) 39 M.L.R. 162.

[17] *Ibid.* at p. 162.

[18] J.M. McLoughlin, *op. cit.* at p. 112.

[19] W. G. Carson, "The Institutionalization of Ambiguity: Early British Factory Acts", in G. Geis and E. Stotland (eds.), *White-Collar Crime: Theory and Research* (1980), pp. 142–73 at p. 162.

[20] *Ibid.* p. 166.

[21] W. G. Carson, "Some Sociological Aspects of Strict Liability and the Enforcement of Factory Legislation", (1979) 33 M.L.R. 396.

[22] Law Commission, W.P. No. 30.

[23] It does, however, apply in effect to the undischarged bankrupt who obtains credit; the offence is one of strict liability, as to which see *Rex* v. *Duke of Leinster* [1924] 1 K.B. 311, but the bankrupt is always notified of the disabilities attaching to his status.

[24] P. Halnan, "Diversion and Decriminalization of Road Traffic Offences" [1978] Crim.L.R. 456.

[25] Road Traffic Bill (Lords), Sess. 1961–62, Standing Committee E, col. 266.

[26] Road Traffic Act 1972, s.93; for a discussion, see B. Harris, *The Criminal Jurisdiction of Magistrates* (7 ed., 1979), ch. 20; note that this is to be replaced by Transport Act 1981, s.19.

[27] Remarks of Lord Rosslyn in Sess. 1903, 125 H.L. Deb. (IV Ser.), col. 537.

[28] Royal Commission on Transport, First Report, *The Control of Traffic on Roads,* 1929, Cmd. 3365, para. 21–25.

[29] See B. Harris, *op. cit.,* pp. 302–303.

[30] An earlier, but very similar account, is contained in my "Aspects of the Control of Economic Crime in the United Kingdom" in *Economic Crime in Europe* (ed. L.H. Leigh 1980), pp. 22–25.

[31] Report of the Committee on Safety and Health at Work, Cmnd. 5019 (1972).

[32] Health and Safety Commission, *Report,* 1977–78, p. 21.

[33] Health and Safety Commission, *Report,* 1979–80, p. 1.

[34] Health and Safety Commission, *Report,* 1976–77, p. 18.

[35] See Health and Safety Executive, *Manufacturing and Service Industries,* 1978, Tables 6, 7 and 8.

[36] Health and Safety Commission, *Report,* 1977–78, p. 22.

[37] Department of the Environment, *Central Unit on Environmental Pollution, Pollution Control in Great Britain: How It works* (2 ed., 1978).

[38] *E.g.* Southern Water Authority, *Annual Report and Accounts,* 1979–80, para. 79; Yorkshire Water Authority, *First Statutory Annual Report and Accounts* (1975), para. 6.13.

[39] Health and Safety Executive, *Industrial Air Pollutions,* (1979), pp. 1–3.

[40] On annual figures for prosecutions see *e.g.* Annual Report of the Director-General of Fair Trading.

[41] Unsolicited Goods and Services Acts 1971–75.

Chapter 6

REFLECTIONS AND CONCLUSIONS

1. *"True Crime," Guilt and Stigma*

This essay has stressed the place of strict and vicarious liability in relation to public welfare offences; to what might be thought of as administrative criminal law. It has not, save inferentially, touched upon the moral significance of the *mens rea* principle and therefore of the place of strict liability generally in the criminal law. It has, thus, not touched upon the debate whether *mens rea* should be retained as a general principle of the criminal law. That question raises issues outside the scope of this essay. There is, however, a question whether there is an area of true crime to which strict liability cannot be admitted. This question seems to me to be essentially spurious.

Professors Fitzgerald and Brett argue forcibly that *mens rea* is a principle which reflects a morality essential to the criminal law. From this it follows that strict (and in this aspect vicarious) liability is admissible only in respect of offences not criminal in character, that is, the category denominated as quasi-criminal, or regulatory offences. Elsewhere, it is impermissible. This suggests a contrast which is ultimately unsustainable.

The contrast posed by those who believe in an absolute demarcation depends upon the notion that the harms involved in crime on the one hand and regulatory offences on the other are different in kind. Thus crimes are said to violate fundamental rules, to constitute wrongs of greater generality, and thus to involve harms of a more obvious kind, than do regulatory offences.[1] The argument proceeds by example. Murder, we are told, contravenes a basic rule essential to the very existence and continuance of human society. Illegal parking violates a useful but not essential rule. Offences are not so general; they are, it is

said, wrongs that are committed when playing certain
special roles. One expects to find them in certain
specialised Codes. Crimes are more obvious wrongs.
Murder and robbery present direct, immediate and clearly
apparent harm to identifiable victims; in the case of
offences, harms are less direct, collective rather than
individual, and often done by carelessness rather than
design. But even supporters of this view recognise that the
harm done by regulatory offences may outweigh that
presented by some traditional crimes. Indeed, for this
reason among others, some moral philosophers deny that
any theory which segregates certain offences from crime
as *mala prohibita* or purely penal in nature is sustainable.[2]
That, however, is not, so we are assured, a reason for
jettisoning the distinction. There is an underlying reality
to the distinction which corresponds to popular belief;
conviction for crime stigmatises a man in a way in which
conviction for a regulatory offence does not. Offences are
more detailed in what they forbid and more arbitrary in
their content than are crimes.

The argument proceeds further. Criminal liability and
punishment is said to be justified only if two conditions are
met; first that the law must not forbid conduct in which a
citizen has a moral right to engage, and secondly, that it
should not penalise those who are known to be without
fault because they had no reasonable chance to comply
with the law's provisions, that is, it should not penalise
those who did not break the law by choice. *Mens rea*
doctrines are essential to personal liberty; they ensure,
partly at least, that persons are not made criminal who do
not meet the conditions outlined above.

With some aspects of these arguments, it is difficult to
agree. One practical matter should at once be stressed; in
English law not only is fault considered when determining
whether to prosecute, but it is also embodied in a wide
range of statutory defences to infractions. Over much of
English law, liability is not strict at all, at least in the sense
that an offender who is free from fault must be convicted.

It may be that the conditions required to make out the defence are onerous, but they are generally not impossible to fulfil. And even in areas where a scheme of defences is not provided, the courts have begun to intervene on the side of the subject. Thus, the common liability which the system presents is liability for fault, with the conditions of defence fairly minutely laid out in legislation. On examination, the novelty in much legislation is that the defendant is placed under a positive burden to make out a defence. This is, of course, more onerous than would be the burden on an accused who wished for example, to raise automatism to a crime of homicide; he would have to make it a live issue and the ultimate burden would rest upon the prosecution.[3] But it is not far removed from that mode of proceeding. On examination, the real question appears to be one of what are the limits to the propositions embodied in *Woolmington's* case[4]; that is, that the prosecution must prove guilt beyond a reasonable doubt. There are, it is true, offences for which no such defences or defences limited to cases of emergency are provided. The penalities imposed, in particular in respect of some pollution offences are not minor. Neither is the harm that such offences present. It is, however, fair to point out both that the harm is preventable by the persons caught by the legislation, and that the instances of severity appear to be instances in which it would be extremely difficult to disprove spurious defences. But, in general, we have arrived at a regime of fault which, based on statute, exculpates the diligent and careful defendant. That does not mean either that improvements cannot be effected to the system, or that a general standard for the construction of legislation is not desirable. It does indicate that basic values are in fact very often embodied in modern legislation.

What this suggests is that both the fault principle and its precise expression depend more upon questions of emphasis and practicality than upon rigid distinctions between phenomena variously labelled as crime or, on the other hand, quasi-crime, regulatory offences, public welfare offences or administrative offences. The question generally only presents itself as one of emphasis outside what may be thought of as the traditional criminal law, but even here, as we have seen, strict liability was imposed for practical reasons, and positive defences provided in order to mitigate its rigours by enabling the careful and diligent individual to escape conviction. We need only recall the examples of crimes of bigamy,[5] sexual intercourse with a girl under sixteen[6] and possession of narcotics.[7] That is not, however, to say that I agree with the details of the traditional argument. Murder can, no doubt, be contrasted with illegal parking, but is it clear that theft necessarily poses a graver violation of a basic rule than does the pollution of a beach in a resort which depends upon its summer trade for prosperity? Is theft necessarily graver than driving a vehicle which has defective brakes or is uninsured? Is assault necessarily worse then reckless driving?

The point is not that some rules embody values more fundamental than others, but rather that the argument for a distinction between crimes and regulatory offences ignores a very difficult problem of demarcation which I doubt can be resolved by invoking exclusively either moral principles or functional considerations. No doubt one could resolve the problem by legislative classification, but that would be simply to shift basic questions to an earlier stage in the process of law-making and enforcing.

The notion of solving these problems by classification is, of course, prominent in academic writing, and is found in the *Model Penal Code* as well, where it is suggested that those offences for which the maximum penalty is a fine be classified as violations, which could attract strict liability together with civil penalties such as forfeitures and cancellations of permits to do business.[8] The late Professor Brett argued that strict liability ought to be imposed only in respect of civil offences by which he meant offences punishable by fine only without the possibility of imprisonment.[9] Such classifications operate in Germany[10] and in Belgium in respect of offences which may attract vicarious liability.[11] But one may question how persuasive this approach would be in the United Kingdom. In the first place, as a purely practical matter, it poses the problem of recasting the statute book in order to remove the possibility of imprisonment from a wide range of statutory offences which generally provide both a fine and possible imprisonment for summary offences. Secondly, it seems to concede the justice of a category of wrongs for which strict liability without affirmative defences may readily be accepted. Even if this is not intended to exclude defences, it places the emphasis in the wrong place and could lead one to the conclusion that minor injustices here can be accepted in the interests of law enforcement. This is, I think, a bad emphasis; injustice ought not to be accepted simply because an infraction is not regarded as serious. In all cases we ought to ask whether defences can be provided and on what terms. In the third place, it seems improbable that a person, convicted of a strict liability offence without being obviously at fault, for example where not even negligence can be proved against him, would be imprisoned. The average minor offender is simply fined. The general run of motoring offenders do not even face the stigma of an appearance in court; they plead guilty by letter. Andenaes, speaking of the continental doctrine of the personal nature of punishment; states:[12]

> "Perhaps the axiom that punishment cannot be imposed without subjective guilt has been carried too far. A fine which may not be converted into imprisonment acts only as a purely economic obligation, comparable to a duty to pay damages or make redress. And if such an economic sanction is a suitable method for the prevention of certain offences, there can hardly be any decisive arguments against it."

The same considerations ought surely to apply where the penalty commonly imposed in cases where no fault is found is a fine.

Is it clear that a person who commits a strict liability offence ought always to escape prison, even where he has been guilty of fault? The answer must surely be not. The repeated motoring offender is more likely to be disqualified than imprisoned, unless he is at fault, and even then imprisonment is usually reserved for those who blatantly breach the prohibition against driving while intoxicated. Such people deserve to be imprisoned. Should a factory owner who fails, whether wilfully or negligently, to obey an enforcement notice be spared imprisonment? Why refrain from imprisoning a person responsible for pollution on the consideration that the offence is one of strict liability where it is clear that he was at fault? The classification of the offence ought not, surely, to be decisive on the issue of sentence, even though the severity of the maximum penalty available is a consideration taken into account in classifying the offence as one requiring *mens rea*? And if the offence is one for which it is difficult to formulate workable defences without subverting enforcement as is the case with many motoring offences, there is no real possibility of a jail sentence for the offender.

This, in turn, taken together with other problems which beset the traditional argument, ought to lead us to view the problem differently. We cannot sustain abstract, categorical distinctions; some crimes have no immediate impact on particular individuals whom we can visualise or who the accused visualises in advance. Stock Exchange rigging is an obvious example; insider trading is another. The former would no doubt be regarded as a true crime, the latter might well not. Lives may be lost by carelessness as well as by design; the law of manslaughter has long penalised persons who kill others by criminally negligent acts or omissions.[13] Strict liability offences are, it is true, often concerned with the details of regulation of an industry or activity; it is by no means clear that they are created arbitrarily. The fact that the prosecution need not prove *mens rea* initially does not make them so, and few, surely, represent legislative whim or caprice. It may be suggested that the classification of offences and the precise limits to strict liability are uncertain, but that is not a particularly convincing reason for condemning strict liability altogether. The limits to liability for theft are also uncertain, especially given the uncertainty and variability of the key concept of dishonesty.[14] To say that the law ought not to forbid a man to do that which he has a moral right to do, and should not penalise those who did not break the law by choice, is at once to state two truisms and beg important questions. The former serves no doubt as a rough guide to the legislature; the latter does not dictate where and how in the criminal process the question of the defendant's fault ("choice" is rather too narrow a conception here) ought to be accommodated.

In short, the relevant questions ought not to be approached from the vantage point of abstract classifications. We ought, rather, to recognise the value of punishing only where there is fault, which may be intention, recklessness or negligence, whether affirmatively or negatively expressed. What mental state is to be required may well, indeed must be, determined with regard to such matters as the gravity of the harm, the nature of the social duty violated, the penalty provided, and the stigma involved. These considerations, taken with problems of enforceability, dictate the terms of statutory schemes of enforcement

There is, thus, no category of offences of a nature to which fault does not apply. Instead, we need, given the general desirability of accommodating fault, to work out the extent and manner of its expression from case to case. But this is a tendency already evident in statutory offences. It needs to be systematised and extended. Furthermore, there is a strong argument that doctrines concerning mistakes of law ought to be re-assessed. In an

era of increasingly complicated law, it seems hard that
ignorance of the law should never be a mistake. Admittedly, persons who are active in regulated industries ought
to know the rules which apply specially to them, but there
is, as we have noted, a case for recognising reasonable
mistakes of law, especially where the defendant has relied
on legal advice, properly given. This is a topic which,
while mentioned in American literature, has scarcely been
addressed here at all.[15]

Apart from such questions as these, there is the vexed
question whether legislative schemes ought to be dealt
with through the criminal courts. It has been argued that
matters of administrative regulation ought to be dealt with
by administrative processes including administrative tri-
bunals. The use of criminal courts to punish petty
infractions is said, somehow, to debase the currency; to
lower respect for the criminal law.[16]

There are, no doubt, considerations of a pragmatic sort
which dictate that reliance should continue to be placed
on the criminal courts as one of the forums where such
legislation is administered. That does not mean that
criminal proceedings, at least those which tend to conviction, ought to be the primary weapon of enforcement, nor
are they so at present. Warnings, exhortations, compliance notices, closure of premises and forfeiture are all
now employed, and many do not require a magisterial
order. Nor is it necessarily the case that the most serious
infractions should be dealt with criminally. Injunction
proceedings, or statutory variations of them, may well be
better adapted to cope with repeated infractions of
legislation, particularly where fines are regarded as a kind
of licensee fee. But we should beware of forgoing recourse
to the cheap, swift and simple procedure of the magistrates' courts from considerations of a dogmatic character.
Magisterial procedures are well-developed and fair. Civil
liberties guarantees are embedded in the system. There is
no need for a system incorporating the beguiling simplici-
ties said to be a desirable attribute of administrative

procedures. We have used magisterial procedures as part of a bundle of controls for a very long time, virtually since the beginning of modern administrative regulation through the various Clauses Acts without obvious ill effects.

In any event, dogmatic arguments are curiously unconvincing. It cannot, surely, be argued that we regard burglars indulgently because many thousands of people are convicted of motoring offences before the criminal courts. Many of them probably suspected their guilt despite their vehement denials to the contrary. How many undergraduates, for example, have taken a chance with a mechanically defective automobile? Equally, it cannot be said that we regard a person convicted of a parking offence as a grave offender because thieves are openly sentenced in the same courts. In short, the public is perfectly capable of making common sense distinctions and does so. That does not mean that magisterial procedures are always the best or even a good procedure in any given case; it does mean that the precise bundle of procedures used can be determined by pragmatic considerations and that it is not necessary to effect a radical transformation in procedures to do justice in the field of administrative criminal law.

Criminal proceedings no doubt provide a valuable adjunct to other administrative controls. In some instances they may well prove to be a swift and reasonably inexpensive deterrent, especially when administrators have tried other methods without success. They may also be used to mould morality in a way that it would be difficult to do otherwise. Furthermore, there are areas where it would be difficult to devise a sanction more suited to the case than a fine; the occasional infraction by a retailer for example where it calls for action, is probably best met thus, and one really would gain nothing by placing the power to punish in a body other than that of the existing magistrates courts. Whether as a primary or ancillary weapon, criminal procedures and sanctions are cheap, useful and, in my submission, quite as just and efficacious as any other machinery which we are likely to devise.

Of course that does not mean that the system cannot be and should not be improved. We need, for example, much greater certainty in interpretation than historically we have had. Admittedly, many problematic cases have been solved by the case law, not always satisfactorily, but there will remain doubtful cases where it is not clear whether strict and vicarious liability are intended. In 1978 the Law Commission suggested legislation to deal with the problem.[17] It would be partly prospective in character, and would apply to new legislation unless that legislation expressly excluded it. Where key words such as intention, knowledge and recklessness were used, the legislation would apply standard tests to them; for example, the standard test of recklessness would involve awareness of risk or of circumstance producing risk, coupled with whether it would be reasonable for the person to take that risk. New offences would use these key words, and the use of other words would be avoided where possible in the description of mental states in legislation. New legislation should expressly state to what extent liability depends on intention, knowledge or recklessness, or on an objective standard of conduct, or is intended to be strict. Furthermore, where there is no provision for fault or for strict liability in relation to any future offence, there would be a presumption that liability depends on intention or recklessness as to any result of conduct and knowledge or recklessness as to any circumstances. No such presumption would operate where the statute provided liability for negligence, or liability regardless of the accused's state of mind, or liability where the defendant's conduct fits an objective state of facts, subject to an affirmative defence. In a novel suggestion, the Law Commission proposes, again in respect of prospective statutes, that where liability is subject to a defence which does not make liability depend on the presence or absence of a particular state of mind, or compliance with an objective standard of conduct, then the defendant should not be liable if he believed in the existence of any circumstance which, had it existed, would have provided him with a defence to or exception from liability. The Law Commission had in mind *Brooks* v. *Mason*[18] where the offence was knowingly selling intoxicating liquor to a minor except in a corked or sealed vessel. The fact that the defendant did not know the bottle to be uncorked and unsealed was not a defence. The Law Commission wished to cover such a case as this where the mental state required for the exception is not specified; in other words, there should be a presumption as to the mental element required for the exception, subject to a persuasive burden on the defendant. The scheme also concerns mistake of fact and proof of *mens rea*.

Such a scheme would no doubt assist courts in the interpretation of legislation. No one, viewing cases like *Caldwell*, could deny that courts do not discharge the task of interpretation with entire consistency.[19] So far as legislation which is silent concerning the requisite mental state is concerned, such a provision would emphasise a trend which recent decisions such as *Sweet* v. *Parsley*[20] appear firmly to have established. The proposal for a presumption in favour of *mens rea* where an existing statute does not use the key words noted above, is intended to give greater consistency in interpretation than now exists. The Law Commission seeks some *prima facie* rule to deal with elusive concepts such as "causing", "permitting" and "possession". Its recommendations deal only with strict liability; no suggestions have as yet been formulated to deal with vicarious liability.

Another reform which might be suggested is the introduction by statute or common law of a general due diligence defence. The desirability of such a change is emphasised in Professor Howard's work. There are, as we have noted, problems with such a suggestion. In the first place, it would have to live with existing statutory schemes, most of which address with some particularity the conditions upon which it is desired to exempt offenders from liability. Any general defence would necessarily have to be subordinate to detailed schemes which addressed the particular problems involved in regulating an activity. Even at present, certain defences have been said, whether rightly or not, to have a distinctly adverse effect on enforcement. For example the defence under pollution legislation that the best practicable means of compliance had been adopted was stringently criticised in Parliamentary debates on clean air legislation.[21] A generally worded defence would produce enforcement problems if it were sought to make it cover the whole ground. Then, too, problems could arise with motoring offences unless such defences were carefully circumscribed; there is much to be said for the motorist being made a virtual insurer of the condition of his vehicle. It may of course be argued that the sentencing judge must in any event inquire into fault in sentencing, but in motoring cases where a virtual tariff of fines applies in practice, that argument is essentially spurious. In the matter of road traffic, where the dangers are great, and the issue is whether the motorist took due care to maintain his vehicle, or to drive prudently, or to ensure that his licence was valid, there is much to be said for the pragmatic, if apparently harsh, position now reached by the courts.

A third reform is to continue the present trend of consolidating affirmative statutory defences under standardised wording. This probably invites a drafting exercise directed towards particular statutory schemes, since wording applicable in one area will probably not apply readily to all. The conditions which have to be satisfied if the defence is to succeed need to be looked at again. In particular, the relationship between the liability of the actual offender, the person who committed the *actus reus*, and the person to whose fault the prohibited state of affairs was fundamentally due, perhaps a manufacturer, needs to be considered so that the burden of liability will not fall primarily upon a mere cog. One must be wary of unwise generalisation; practical problems of law enforcement are often not within the knowledge of an academic writer. But one would like to know the practical impact of the third party procedure in for example s.27 of the Weights and Measures Act 1963, and how often and in what circumstances it is short-circuited by s.27(4). In short, to what extent is it necessary to make an accused person prove the guilt of another as the price of his own exculpation? Here, no doubt, is the stuff of which a good empirical study could be made.

The problem of vicarious liability is a difficult one. It is hard to see what canons of interpretation might be devised to assist the court. In any event, the question whether vicarious liability should be imposed for strict liability offences appears not to produce grave problems in practice. It is difficult to see a justification for vicarious liability for *mens rea* offences, at any rate outside the Licensing Acts. There is, here, a hidden problem, at any rate if one regards personal corporate criminal liability as a disguised form of vicarious liability for one then arrives at the conclusion that in practice, in respect of legal persons and bodies assimilated to them by statute, a measure of vicarious liability for traditional offences is admitted where it would not be if a natural person were the accused. This is not the place to pursue that problem, but we do need to know in respect of what conduct a supervisory duty can be placed upon individuals who can be convicted of criminal offences in respect of them.[22] The answer may well be to maintain traditional criminal liability in cases of fraud, for example, but also to create by their side what are essentially administrative offences in somewhat wider terms, to which duties of supervision, criminally enforceable, can attach.[23] There seems no reason why we should not use administrative offences, that is, offences of strict liability, for defaults of this sort, reserving for the traditional criminal law offences involving moral fault which can be used where the fault is both grave and provable for those who actively participate in the offence.

If one were to attempt a balance sheet or other summary of the status of strict and vicarious liability in English criminal law, one would have first to concede that its existence, over a wide range of infractions, is a practical necessity. The growth of regulatory legislation, aided by increasingly sophisticated technology, makes it impossible in many cases to prove the defendant's mental state from the act done, even tentatively. One could hardly presume, from the fact that a merchant sold milk deficient in butterfat, that he or the manufacturer was necessarily aware of or reckless as to this circumstance, or even negligent in respect of processing prior to sale. But, equally, it seems clear that conflict in the case law exists, and that it cannot always convincingly be explained by reference to such considerations. No one has as yet convincingly explained why in *Sherras* v. *de Rutzen*[24] supplying liquor to a constable on duty should attract *mens rea*, while selling liquor to an intoxicated person in *Cundy* v. *Le Coq*[25] was an offence of strict liability, nor why in *Prince's* case there should have been strict liability as to the age of the girl whereas in *Tolson mens rea* was required for the offence despite the presence of particularised affirmative defences. As to the former brace of cases, Professor Howard is surely right to contend that there is but the most trivial distinction between them.[26] Certainly, the discrepancies in result in these and many other cases cannot convincingly be explained by reference to the exigencies of enforcement. It surely is no more difficult or easy to prove that a person knew the age of a nubile young woman to prove the state of mind of someone concerning whether a missing spouse is alive or dead.

One would have next to inquire to what extent the injustices inherent in strict and vicarious liability are mitigated by statute, by the courts and by the administration. Here, there has been a distinct change in judicial thinking; recent decisions have strongly reiterated the common law presumption of *mens rea*. Furthermore, in road traffic at least, conceptions of no fault have begun to operate, albeit in a fragmented way. But much more important has been the continuing elaboration and refinement of affirmative defences. These, coupled with a wide measure of discretion on the part of enforcement authorities, do much to minimise injustice in the operation of the law. Plainly, they do not cover the whole ground. If we have not as yet avoided subjecting the "blameless harmdoer" to the risk of criminal conviction, we have at least gone a long way towards reconciling his interest in individual justice with the need to protect the public against a variety of evils associated primarily with carrying on particular trades and industries.

We ought further to consider what improvements could be made to the system. The Law Commission's initiative has been discussed above. We have ventured suggestions concerning defences. Other ideas, such as creating a category of lesser offences perhaps called "violations" to which strict liability might apply, do not, as I have noted, seem helpful to me. One has, in any event, to decide what conduct should fall within that category and why.[27] In the result, while one might effect a change of label, I cannot see that any improvement of substance, either in enforcement of the law or doing justice in the particular case, is likely to result. It may be urged that relegating such conduct to a lesser category would avoid social stigma on the one hand, and a debasing of the verbal currency of the notion of crime on the other. But in the first place some offences of strict liability should carry a stigma, for example pollution, and in the second place, I have no doubt that the public does make the appropriate distinctions. Nor would abandonment of criminal law and procedure as a mode of control, among others, seem desirable. On the other hand, there is much to be said for its invocation as a last resort, and for the development and utilisation of a bundle of other controls, such as seizures, closure orders, improvement notices, warnings, and, the like; in short for continuing enforcement trends which are now evident and some of which, indeed, have been evident for a very long time.

The Law Reform Commission of Canada suggests that criminal liability and punishment are only justified provided that two conditions are met: first that the law must not be oppressive and forbid things that the citizen has a moral right to do and should be free to do; and secondly that it should not penalise those who are known to be without fault because they had no reasonable chance to comply with its provision.[28] The first of these criteria raises issues of a character too broad for consideration here; as to the second, perhaps the dictates of justice are better recognised both in law and practice than conventional accounts might suggest. In any event, administrative criminal law provides a subject for inquiry much wider and more interesting than a mere study of some of the leading cases would suggest.

NOTES

[1] The summary of Professor Fitzgerald's argument derives from Law Reform Commission of Canada, *Strict Liability* (1974) , chapter 1. The moral arguments are also put by Colin Howard, *Strict Responsibility* (1963), although not in quite the same way, for Professor Brett, see P. Brett, "Strict Responsibility: Possible Solutions", (1974) 37 M.L.R. 417.

[2] T. E. Davitt, *The Elements of Law* (1959) pp. 189–191, cited in W. Childress, *Civil Disobedience and Political Obligation* (1971), p. 179.

[3] *e.g. per* Lord Denning in *Bratty* v. *A.G. for Northern Ireland* [1963] A.C. 386; see also *Reg.* v. *Dix* (1981) 74 Cr.App.R. 307.

[4] *Per* Lord Diplock in *Sweet* v. *Parsley* [1970] A.C. 312.

[5] Offences Against The Person Act 1861, s.57.

[6] Sexual Offences Act 1956, s.6.

[7] Misuse of Drugs Act 1971, s.5.

[8] A.L.I. *Model Penal Code,* s.2.02; for a discussion, see C. Howard, *op. cit.,* chap. 8.

[9] P. Brett, "Strict Responsibility: Possible Solutions", (1974) 37 M.L.R. 417.

[10] R. Screvens, "Les Sanctions Applicables aux Personnes Morales", in *La Responsibilità Penale Delle Persone Giuridiche in Diritto Communitario* (University of Messina, 1980), at pp. 179–180.

[11] P. Delatte, "La Responsibilité Pénale Des Personnes Morales", *ibid.* at pp. 289–292.

[12] J. Andenaes, *The General Part of the Criminal Law of Norway* (1965) p. 241.

[13] *Rex* v. *Bateman* (1925) 19 Cr.App.R. 8.

[14] *e.g. R.* v. *Feely* [1973] 1 Q.B. 530; *Boggeln* v. *Williams* [1978] 2 All E.R. 1061; *Reg.* v. *McIvor*, [1982] 1 W.L.R. 409.

[15] G.P. Fletcher, *Rethinking Criminal Law* (1978) pp. 716–758; Bill S.1722, s.501, a proposal to amend the United States Code would continue in vigour reasonable mistake of law, in existing legislation. For particular formulations—for example conduct taken after obtaining official advice, see American Law Institute, *Model Penal Code*, s.609, *Federal Securities Code*, s.1517(*b*)(3). s.1517(*c*)(3) of the latter would eliminate any possibility of imprisoning a person who acted in ignorance of regulations, rather than of the code itself. For an English account, see A. J. Ashworth, *loc. cit.*

[16] J. D. Morton, The Function of Criminal law in 1962 (C.B.C. 1962).

[17] The Law Commission, *Report on the Mental Element in Crime* (Law Com. No.89), (1978); J.C. Smith and B. Hogan, *Criminal Law: Cases and Materials* (2 ed., 1980) pp. 97–102 contains a convenient summary.

[18] [1902] 2 K.B. 743.

[19] [1981] 2 W.L.R. 509.

[20] [1970] A.C 132.

[21] Sess. 1956–57, 551 H.C. Deb. (Vth) Ser. cols. 127 ff.

[22] I have alluded to the matter in "The Criminal Liability of Corporations and Other Groups" (1977) *Ottawa L.Rev.* 247.

[23] Some of these developments are summarised, in the context of corporate liability (in French) by R. Screvens, "Les Sanctions Applicables Aux Personnes Morales", in *La Responsibilità Penale Delle Persone Giuridiche in Diritto Communitario.*

[24] [1895] 1 Q.B. 918.

[25] (1884) 13 Q.B.D. 207.

[26] C. Howard, *Strict Responsibility* (1963), p. 8, n. 1.

[27] This, suggestion is a prominent feature of the American Law Institute, *Model Penal Code* (1962); for a full account, see C. Howard, *Strict Responsibility* (1963), ch. 8.

[28] Law Reform Commission of Canada, *Studies on Strict Liability* (1974), Part 1, p. 5.

INDEX